Published by North Parade Publishing Ltd.
4 North Parade Bath, England.

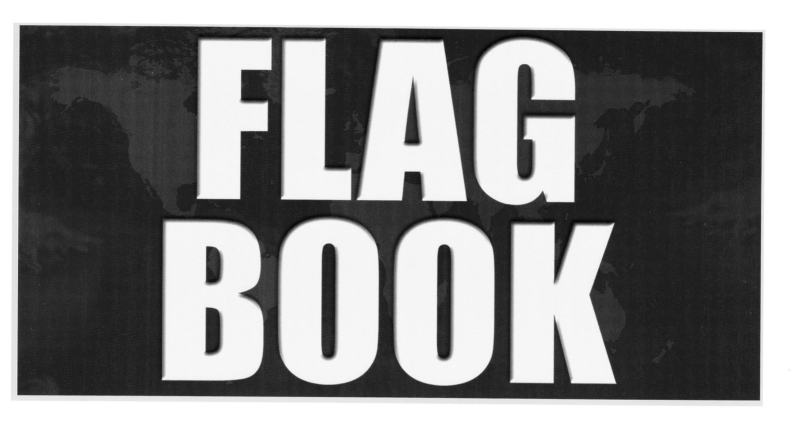

# CONTENTS

**Chinese flag**

**Indian *dhvaja***

**Islamic flag**

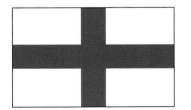

**Cross of St George**

**Kyrenia crusader flag**

In ancient times, it was the flag that told one if the approaching individual was a friend or foe. The flag also helped a discouraged army to renew the fight with spirit.

Those battle flags were first devised by the Chinese and the Indians. It is believed that, as far back as 1122 BC, the founder of China's Chou Dynasty travelled with a white-coloured flag as his emblem. The royal flag was identified with the prestige of the king's office and it was considered a crime to show it any disrespect. The fall of the flag would signify defeat for the king and, hence, its protection was entrusted to an able general. Standard motifs in Chinese flags included the blue dragon, the red bird and the white tiger.

Indian flags commonly featured a figure designed in golden shades and fringe, against a scarlet or green background. The shape was often triangular. The flags were usually mounted on chariots or elephants, especially during a battle.

In contrast, Islamic flags were one plain colour – black, white, or red. This was because Islam disallowed the usage of any known image. Over the course of time green, which was the colour of the 10th-century-AD Fatimid Dynasty, was adopted by Islam.

Europe took its own time to embrace the idea of the flag. In the Middle Ages, leaders began using the flag of their patron saint to represent their country – for instance, the Cross of St George (white with a red cross) was widely used in 13th-century England. The oldest European flags still in use are those with the Christian cross, which was widely used in the Crusades – military wars fought against Muslims in the 11th-13th centuries.

By the end of the Middle Ages, flags became the standard symbols of nations, cities, organisations and guilds. They also began to find uses for signalling and for decoration and display. Special meanings came to be associated with particular types and colours of flags. The white flag has been used as a universal signal for peace. Similarly, the black flag became the symbol of pirates and, later, of mourning.

Over time, nations adopted flags to represent themselves. The colours and designs of these flags go back a long time – to the history, culture, values and struggles of a particular country and era.

The study of the various aspects of flags is known as vexillology (from the Latin *vexillum*, meaning 'banner'). Some sources assert it was the Roman Empire's *vexillum* that was the first 'true' flag.

Roman *vexillum*

# TYPES OF FLAGS

The colours in a flag follow a 'fixed and ordered pattern', and certainly cannot be altered as and when one wishes. A flag's colours usually have a history behind their adoption and bear distinct meanings. Flags are usually rectangular, though one sees flags in squares, pennants, swallowtails and other shapes too. The flag of Nepal is, in fact, a combination of two triangular forms!

Typically, designs on flags are crosses, stripes, stars and divisions of the surface (field) into bands. Flags are mainly distinguished by their respective national symbols. Flags may also feature different designs on each side, as can be seen on several flags of the U.S. states.

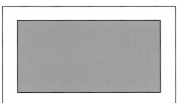

Border

Bicolour

Tricolour

Quartered

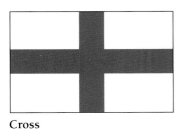

Cross

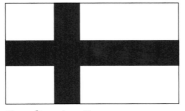

Scandinavian Cross

Saltire

Couped Cross

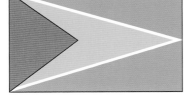

Triangle

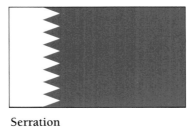

Fimbriation

Serration

# NORTH AND CENTRAL AMERICA

Canada, the second largest country in the world, takes up nearly two-fifths of the North American continent. Canada and the United States share a border about 8,895 kilometres (5,527 miles) long. Another country sharing a common border with the United States is Mexico. The world's largest island, Greenland, lies in the North Atlantic Ocean. Two-thirds of the island falls within the Arctic Circle and over 80 per cent of the surface is ice-capped.

## BELIZE

**Adopted on:** September 21, 1981
**Ratio:** 3:5
**Capital:** Belmopan
**Independence from the United Kingdom:** September 21, 1981
**What it means:** The blue is the colour of the main political party, People's United Party (PUP), while the red represents the opposition United Democratic Party (UDP). The national coat of arms is featured in the middle.

## CANADA

**Adopted on:** February 15, 1965
**Ratio:** 1:2
**Capital:** Ottawa
**Independence (union of British North American colonies):** July 1, 1867
**What it means:** Red and white are the national colours of Canada. The maple leaf at the centre is a national symbol.

## COSTA RICA

**Adopted on:** September 29, 1848
**Ratio:** 3:5
**Capital:** San Jose
**Independence from Spain:** September 15, 1821
**What it means:** Blue and white are the original colours used by the United Provinces of Central America. The red, white and blue at the bottom are inspired by the French tricolour.

## EL SALVADOR

**Adopted on:** May 17, 1912
**Ratio:** 4:7
**Capital:** San Salvador
**Independence from Spain:** September 15, 1821
**What it means:** Blue and white are the original colours used by the United Provinces of Central America. The coat of arms includes the national motto "God, union, liberty".

## GREENLAND

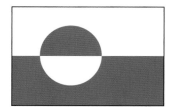

**Adopted on:** June 21, 1985
**Ratio:** 2:3
**Capital:** Nuuk (Godthab)
**Independence:** none; self-governing part of the Kingdom of Denmark
**What it means:** The white stands for the island's ice cap and glaciers, while the red is symbolic of the fjords and the sun.

## GUATEMALA

**Adopted on:** August 17, 1871
**Ratio:** 5:8
**Capital:** Guatemala
**Independence from Spain:** September 15, 1821
**What it means:** Blue and white are the original colours used by the United Provinces of Central America. The coat of arms features the national bird, the quetzal, as a symbol of liberty.

## HONDURAS

**Adopted on:** February 16, 1866
**Ratio:** 1:2
**Capital:** Tegucigalpa
**Independence from Spain:** September 15, 1821
**What it means:** The colours and the five stars represent the United Provinces of Central America.

## MEXICO

**Adopted on:** November 2, 1821
**Ratio:** 4:7
**Capital:** Mexico City
**Independence from Spain:** September 16, 1810
**What it means:** The colours are those of the national liberation army of Mexico. The coat of arms features the badge of Mexico City.

GREENLAND

Nuuk
(Godthab)

CANADA

Ottawa

UNITED STATES OF AMERICA

Washington,
D.C.

MEXICO

Belmopan

Guatemala

Mexico City

BELIZE

Tegucigalpa

HONDURAS

NICARAGUA

GUATEMALA

Managua

San Salvador

EL SALVADOR

PANAMA

San Jose

COSTA RICA

Panama
City

## NICARAGUA

**Adopted on:** September 4, 1908
**Ratio:** 3:5
**Capital:** Managua
**Independence from Spain:** September 15, 1821
**What it means:** The flag features the original colours used by the United Provinces of Central America. The five volcanoes in the coat of arms represent the five original Central American countries.

## PANAMA

**Adopted on:** November 3, 1903
**Ratio:** 2:3
**Capital:** Panama City
**Independence from Colombia:** November 3, 1903; from Spain on November 28, 1821
**What it means:** Modelled on the U.S. flag, the red and blue originally represented the Liberal and Conservative parties, respectively. White symbolises peace.

## UNITED STATES OF AMERICA

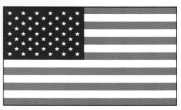

**Adopted on:** July 4, 1960
**Ratio:** 10:19
**Capital:** Washington, D.C.
**Independence from Great Britain:** July 4, 1776
**What it means:** The 50 stars represent the 50 states of the Union, while the 13 stripes stand for the 13 original states.

# SOUTH AMERICA

L ocated between the Pacific and Atlantic oceans, the continent of South America is roughly triangular in shape. It is the fourth largest continent. Mount Aconcagua in Argentina is the continent's highest point. Argentina also boasts the continent's lowest point – the Valdés Peninsula.

GUYANA
Georgetown
Caracas
SURINAME
Paramaribo
VENEZUELA
Cayenne
Bogot
ECUADOR
COLOMBIA
FRENCH GUIANA
Quito

PERU
BRAZIL
Lima
BOLIVIA
Brasilia
La Paz

PARAGUAY
CHILE
Asuncion

ARGENTINA
URUGUAY
Santiago
Buenos Aires
Montevideo

FALKLAND ISLANDS
Stanley

## ARGENTINA

**Adopted:** 1812
**Ratio:** 1:2 and 9:14 on land; 2:3 at sea
**Capital:** Buenos Aires
**Independence from Spain:**
July 9, 1816
**What it means:** The 'Sun of May' emblem refers to the events of May 1810, when, just before a battle, General Belgrano, who designed the flag, looked up and saw the clouds part to show the blue sky and the shining sun.

## BOLIVIA

**Adopted:** 1851
**Ratio:** 2:3
**Capital:** La Paz
**Independence from Spain:**
August 6, 1825
**What it means:** Red is said to represent valour, yellow the country's mineral wealth, and green the fertile land.

## BRAZIL

**Adopted:** 1889
**Ratio:** 7:10
**Capital:** Brasilia
**Independence from Portugal:**
September 7, 1822
**What it means:** The green field is a
symbol for Brazil's forests, while the
yellow diamond represents gold.
The blue disc features the motto
'Order and progress'.

## CHILE

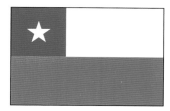

**Adopted:** 1817
**Ratio:** 2:3
**Capital:** Santiago
**Independence from Spain:**
September 18, 1810
**What it means:** Blue is symbolic of
the sky; white stands for the snow on
the Andes Mountains; and red recalls
the blood that was shed in the long
freedom struggle.

## COLOMBIA

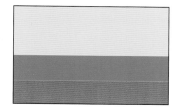

**Adopted:** 1819
**Ratio:** 2:3
**Capital:** Bogotá
**Independence from Spain:**
July 20, 1810
**What it means:** Yellow is said to be
symbolic of sovereignty and justice,
blue of loyalty, and red of courage.

## ECUADOR

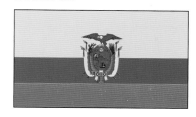

**Adopted:** 1860
**Ratio:** 1:2
**Capital:** Quito
**Independence from Spain:**
May 24, 1822
**What it means:** The colours are
those of the tricolour flown by the
South American revolutionary
Francisco de Miranda.

## FALKLAND ISLANDS

**Adopted:** 1948
**Ratio:** 1:2
**Capital:** Stanley
**Independence:** None; self-governing
territory of the United Kingdom
**What it means:** The ram featured in
the national coat of arms represents
the islands' sheep industry. The U.K.
flag is incorporated on the hoist side.

## FRENCH GUIANA

**Adopted:** --
**Ratio:** 2:3
**Capital:** Cayenne
**Independence:** None; overseas
department of France
**What it means:** Uses the flag
of France.

## GUYANA

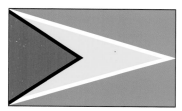

**Adopted:** 1966
**Ratio:** 3:5 on land; 1:2 at sea
**Capital:** Georgetown
**Independence from the United
Kingdom:** May 26, 1966
**What it means:** The yellow triangle
symbolises a bright future; red, the
people's zeal in building the nation;
and black, determination.

## PARAGUAY

**Adopted:** 1842
**Ratio:** 3:5
**Capital:** Asuncion
**Independence from Spain:**
May 14, 1811
**What it means:** The coat of arms
depict the 'Star of May', a symbol of
freedom. The treasury seal on the other
side has the motto 'Peace and justice'.

## PERU

**Adopted:** 1825
**Ratio:** 2:3
**Capital:** Lima
**Independence from Spain:**
July 28, 1821
**What it means:** Red and white are
associated with the ancient Inca
people, who ruled Peru for centuries.
The coat of arms is featured only
when the government uses the flag.

## SURINAME

**Adopted:** 1975
**Ratio:** 2:3
**Capital:** Paramaribo
**Independence from the Netherlands:**
November 25, 1975
**What it means:** The green stripes are
symbolic of the country's forests;
white of justice and freedom; and red
of the spirit of a new nation. The star
represents unity and hope.

## URUGUAY

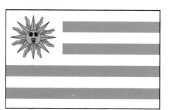

**Adopted:** 1830
**Ratio:** 2:3
**Capital:** Montevideo
**Independence from Brazil:**
August 25, 1825
**What it means:** The nine stripes are
for the nine original departments of
the republic. Like several other South
American countries, the Uruguay flag
features the 'Sun of May'.

## VENEZUELA

**Adopted:** 1836
**Ratio:** 2:3
**Capital:** Caracas
**Independence from Spain:**
July 5, 1811
**What it means:** The arc of seven
stars represents the original seven
provinces that supported the
independence movement.

# THE CARIBBEAN

The Caribbean is a group of islands in the Caribbean Sea, alternatively known as the West Indies. Situated largely on one of the earth's natural plates – known as the Caribbean plate – the area is comprised of more than 7,000 islands and reefs.

THE BAHAMAS
Nassau
TURKS AND CAICOS ISLANDS
Havana
Grand Turk
CUBA
DOMINICAN REPUBLIC
George Town
CAYMAN ISLANDS
HAITI
San Juan
JAMAICA
Santo Domingo
Kingston
Port-au-Prince
PUERTO RICO

## ANTIGUA AND BARBUDA

**Adopted:** 1967
**Ratio:** About 2:3
**Capital:** Saint John's
**Independence from the United Kingdom:** November 1, 1981
**What it means:** The V shape in the centre stands for victory, while the sun symbolises the dawn of a new era.

## THE BAHAMAS

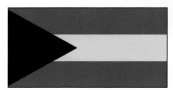

**Adopted:** 1973
**Ratio:** 1:2
**Capital:** Nassau
**Independence from the United Kingdom:** July 10, 1973
**What it means:** The aquamarine stripes are for the waters around the islands; the yellow for the sandy beaches; and the black triangle for the strength of the people.

## BARBADOS

**Adopted:** 1966
**Ratio:** 2:3
**Capital:** Bridgetown
**Independence from the United Kingdom:** November 30, 1966
**What it means:** The blue-yellow-blue stripes stand for sea, sand and sky. The trident head is symbolic of the nation's break from its colonial history.

## CAYMAN ISLANDS

**Adopted:** 1959
**Ratio:** 1:2
**Capital:** George Town
**Independence:** None; overseas territory of the United Kingdom
**What it means:** The three stars in the coat of arms represent the three main islands, while the pineapple and the turtle stand for the flora and fauna.

## CUBA

**Adopted:** 1902
**Ratio:** 1:2
**Capital:** Havana
**Independence from Spain:** December 10, 1898
**What it means:** The red triangle is said to be a symbol for equality, and the white star in it stands for independence.

## DOMINICA

**Adopted:** 1978
**Ratio:** 1:2
**Capital:** Roseau
**Independence from the United Kingdom:** November 3, 1978
**What it means:** The yellow-white-black cross represents the island's original inhabitants. The ring of 10 stars represents the 10 parishes.

## DOMINICAN REPUBLIC

Adopted: 1844
Ratio: 5:8
Capital: Santo Domingo
Independence from Haiti:
February 27, 1844
What it means: The white
cross represents faith. When
used officially, the flag features
the coat of arms bearing the
flag, the Holy Bible and a cross.

## GRENADA

Adopted: 1974
Ratio: 3:5
Capital: Saint George's
Independence from the
United Kingdom:
February 7, 1974
What it means: The outer stars
represent the six parishes and
the central star, the capital.

## GUADELOUPE

Adopted: --
Ratio: 2:3
Capital: Basse-Terre
Independence: None; overseas
department of France
What it means: The flag of
France is used.

## HAITI

Adopted: 1803
Ratio: 3:5
Capital: Port-au-Prince
Independence from France:
January 1, 1804
What it means: The blue and
red are taken from the French
tricolour. The coat of arms is
inscribed with the motto
'Union makes strength'.

ANTIGUA
AND
BARBUDA

Saint John's

sseterre

AINT
ITTS
AND
NEVIS

GUADELOUPE (Fr)

DOMINICA
Roseau

MARTINIQUE (Fr)

SAINT LUCIA
Castries

SAINT
VINCENT
AND THE
GRENADINES

BARBADOS

Bridgetown

GRENADA

Kingstown

Saint George's

Port-of-Spain

TRINIDAD
AND TOBAGO

## JAMAICA

Adopted: 1962
Ratio: 1:2
Capital: Kingston
Independence from the United
Kingdom: August 6, 1962
What it means: the black,
yellow and green represent,
respectively, the difficulties
suffered by the nation, the
shining sun, and the fertile land.

## PUERTO RICO

Adopted: 1922
Ratio: 1:2
Capital: San Juan
Independence: None; self-
governing commonwealth
associated with the United States
What it means: The white
stripes symbolise liberty, and
the red ones and the triangle,
the legislative, executive and
judicial branches of the state.

## SAINT KITTS AND
NEVIS

Adopted: 1983
Ratio: About 2:3
Capital: Basseterre
Independence from the
United Kingdom: September
19, 1983
What it means: The green
triangle represents land and
the red one, years of freedom
struggle. The black symbolises
the islands' African heritage.

## SAINT LUCIA

Adopted: 1967
Ratio: 1:2
Capital: Castries
Independence from the
United Kingdom:
February 22, 1979
What it means: The blue is for
the Caribbean Sea. The
triangles are for the famous
twin peaks of the Pitons.

## SAINT VINCENT AND
THE GRENADINES

Adopted: 1985
Ratio: 2:3
Capital: Kingstown
Independence from the United
Kingdom: October 27, 1979
What it means: The green
diamonds represent the 'Gems
of the Antilles', as the islands
are known. The V shape refers
to the first alphabet in Vincent.

## TRINIDAD AND
TOBAGO

Adopted: 1962
Ratio: 3:5
Capital: Port-of-Spain
Independence from the United
Kingdom: August 31, 1962
What it means: The white
stripes symbolise the sea.
Red represents the vitality
of the people, and black,
their strength.

# WESTERN EUROPE

Western Europe is made up of a widely varying landscape – from Spain, located at the intersection of Europe and Africa, to the island nation of Iceland, which has an abundance of glaciers and geysers. The 'emerald isle' of Ireland boasts an Atlantic coastline with a 3,200-kilometre- (2,000-mile)-wide stretch of ocean.

## ANDORRA

**Adopted:** 1866
**Ratio:** 2:3
**Capital:** Andorra la Vella
**Independence:** 1278
**What it means:** The colours are taken from the flags of France and Spain, which have joint jurisdiction over the principality. The Andorran coat of arms is featured in the centre.

## BELGIUM

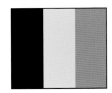

**Adopted:** 1831
**Ratio:** 13:15
**Capital:** Brussels
**Independence from the Netherlands:** October 4, 1830
**What it means:** The colours have been taken from the national coat of arms – black from the shield, gold from the lion, and red from the lion's claws and tongue.

## FRANCE

**Adopted:** 1794
**Ratio:** 2:3
**Capital:** Paris
**Independence:** 843, Treaty of Verdun
**What it means:** The colours stand for the ideals of the 1789 French Revolution – liberty, equality and fraternity.

## ICELAND

**Adopted:** 1915
**Ratio:** 18:25
**Capital:** Reykjavik
**Independence from Denmark:** June 17, 1944
**What it means:** The red is thought to symbolise the volcanoes in the island country. White is for snow and ice, and blue is the bordering Atlantic Ocean. The cross design is based on the Danish flag.

## IRELAND (EIRE)

**Adopted:** 1919
**Ratio:** 1:2
**Capital:** Dublin
**Independence from the United Kingdom:** December 6, 1921
**What it means:** Green is symbolic of the Roman Catholics, orange of the Protestants, and white of peace between the two sects.

## ITALY

**Adopted:** 1919
**Ratio:** 2:3
**Capital:** Rome
**Independence (Kingdom of Italy proclaimed):** March 17, 1861
**What it means:** One legend has it that the green in the flag was used since it was the favourite colour of Napoleon. However, the green and the white might also have been based on the uniforms of the militia of Milan, Italy.

## LUXEMBOURG

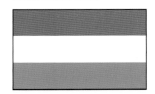

**Adopted:** 1972
**Ratio:** 3:5
**Capital:** Luxembourg
**Independence from the Netherlands:** 1839
**What it means:** The colours go back to the 13th-century coat of arms used by the grand duke.

## MALTA

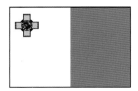

**Adopted:** 1964
**Ratio:** 2:3
**Capital:** Valletta
**Independence from the United Kingdom:** September 21, 1964
**What it means:** The colours were taken from the badge used by the Knights of Malta.

## MONACO

**Adopted:** 1881
**Ratio:** 4:5
**Capital:** Monaco
**Independence (the House of Grimaldi begins its rule):** 1419
**What it means:** The red and white are the heraldic colours of the House of Grimaldi.

## NETHERLANDS, THE

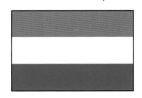

**Adopted:** 1937
**Ratio:** 2:3
**Capital:** Amsterdam
**Independence:** January 23, 1579
**What it means:** The colours were originally taken from the livery colours of William of Orange, a Dutch prince (the orange was later replaced by red).

## PORTUGAL

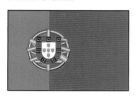

**Adopted:** 1911
**Ratio:** 2:3
**Capital:** Lisbon
**Independence (Kingdom of Portugal recognized):** 1143
**What it means:** Green represents the Portuguese explorer, King Henry the Navigator. Red was the colour of the revolutionary flag. The central shield is symbolic of the country's history of ocean exploration.

## SAN MARINO

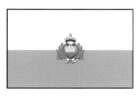

**Adopted:** 1862
**Ratio:** 3:4
**Capital:** San Marino
**Independence (republic founded):** September 3, c. AD 301; treaty with Italy signed in 1862 recognising independence under Italy's protection
**What it means:** White is symbolic of the snow on Mount Titano, the country's highest point, and blue symbolises the sky.

ICELAND
Reykjavik

Northern Ireland
Scotland
UNITED KINGDOM
EIRE
Dublin
England
Wales
London

NETHERLANDS
Amsterdam
BELGIUM
Brussels
LUXEMBOURG
Luxembourg
Paris
SWITZERLAND
FRANCE
Bern

ITALY
SAN MARINO
San Marino
PORTUGAL
Andorra
Monaco
Lisbon
Madrid
MONACO
CORSICA
Rome
SPAIN
ANDORRA
SARDINIA
VATICAN CITY

SICILY

MALTA Valletta

## SPAIN

**Adopted:** 1927
**Ratio:** 2:3
**Capital:** Madrid
**Independence (unification of several independent kingdoms):** 1492
**What it means:** Red and yellow are the original colours of the coat of arms of the Castile and Aragon regions.

## SWITZERLAND

**Adopted:** 1889
**Ratio:** Square in proportion
**Capital:** Bern
**Independence (founding of the confederation):** August 1, 1291
**What it means:** The design is based on the war flag used by the Holy Roman Empire.

## UNITED KINGDOM

**Adopted:** 1801
**Ratio:** 1:2
**Capital:** London
**Independence (current name of the United Kingdom of Great Britain and Northern Ireland adopted):** 1927
**What it means:** The design features three crosses – of St George (England), St Andrew (Scotland) and St Patrick (Ireland).

## VATICAN CITY

**Adopted:** 1929
**Ratio:** Square in proportion
**Capital:** Vatican City
**Independence from Italy:** February 11, 1929
**What it means:** The colours are those of the keys of St Peter's. The emblem itself features the keys upholding the papal crown.

# CENTRAL EUROPE

Central Europe is a loose term applying to those countries lying between Eastern and Western Europe. One of the most recently formed of these is Slovenia. Slovenia has been shaped by limestone plateaus, ridges, caves, underground rivers, valleys and the steep Alpine peaks. There is also a short coastal strip to its southwest. The landscape of Slovakia is marked by the Western Carpathian Mountains. The Alps forms a natural and majestic barrier for the countries of Germany and Austria.

## AUSTRIA

**Adopted:** 1945
**Ratio:** 2:3
**Capital:** Vienna
**Independence (proclaimed republic):**
November 12, 1918
**What it means:** The colours red and white have long been associated with the Austrian legend of the Battle of Acre and the blood-stained white tunic of the war hero, Luitpold V of Badenberg.

## CZECH REPUBLIC

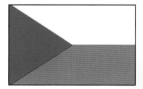

**Adopted:** 1920
**Ratio:** 2:3
**Capital:** Prague
**Independence:** January 1, 1993
(Czechoslovakia split into the Czech Republic and Slovakia)
**What it means:** The stripes are the herladic colours of Bohemia, which make up a large part of the Czech Republic. The blue of the isosceles triangle was used to represent the state of Moravia in the republic.

## DENMARK

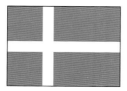

**Adopted in:** 1625 (oldest European flag)
**Ratio:** 28:34 (can be extended to 37)
**Capital:** Copenhagen
**Independence (became a constitutional monarchy):** June 5, 1849
**What it means:** The flag (Dannebrog) is claimed to be a token from the Pope given at the time of the Crusades. The cross design (Scandinavian Cross) was later adopted by other regional flags.

## FINLAND

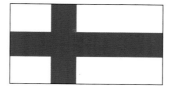

**Adopted:** 1918
**Ratio:** 11:18
**Capital:** Helsinki
**Independence from Russia:** December 6, 1917
**What it means:** The blue is for the thousands of lakes in Finland, and the white for the snow. When flown by the government, the flag has the coat of arms featuring a lion.

## GERMANY

**Adopted:** 1949
**Ratio:** 3:5
**Capital:** Berlin
**Independence (federal republic proclaimed):** May 23, 1949
**What it means:** The colours were taken after the uniforms of German soldiers who fought in the Napoleonic Wars (1804-1815).

## LIECHTENSTEIN

**Adopted:** 1937
**Ratio:** 3:5
**Capital:** Vaduz
**Independence from the Holy Roman Empire:** July 12, 1806
**What it means:** The crown symbolises the independence of the principality. Blue and red respectively stand for the sky and the evening fires at homes.

## NORWAY

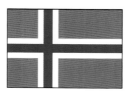

**Adopted:** 1821
**Ratio:** 8:11
**Capital:** Oslo
**Independence (union with Sweden declared dissolved):** June 7, 1905
**What it means:** The tricolour is a symbol of liberty, and influenced by the French, U.K. and U.S. flags. The cross takes after the design of the Danish and Swedish flags.

## POLAND

**Adopted:** 1919
**Ratio:** 5:8
**Capital:** Warsaw
**Independence:** November 11, 1918
**What it means:** The white and red have traditionally been associated with Poland's coat of arms.

## SLOVAKIA

**Adopted:** 1992
**Ratio:** 2:3
**Capital:** Bratislava
**Independence (Czechoslovakia split into the Czech Republic and Slovakia):** January 1, 1993
**What it means:** The flag features the traditional pan-Slavic colours.

## SLOVENIA

**Adopted:** 1991
**Ratio:** 1:2
**Capital:** Ljubljana
**Independence from Yugoslavia:** June 25, 1991
**What it means:** The colours are the traditional pan-Slavic colours used on the flags of the Slavic peoples of Europe. The coat of arms is said to be based on the one used by the duchy of Celje.

## SWEDEN

**Adopted:** 1906
**Ratio:** 5:8
**Capital:** Stockholm
**Independence:** June 6, 1523
**What it means:** The yellow and blue colours are those of the national coat of arms. The cross, again, is designed after the Danish flag.

# EASTERN EUROPE

Geographically, Eastern Europe is marked as the region extending from the Ural and Caucasus mountains in the east to the western border of Russia. Nearly all the countries in this region gained independence only in the 20th century. Russia is the world's largest country, occupying about double the area of the United States!

## ALBANIA

**Adopted on:** April 7, 1992
**Ratio:** 5:7
**Capital:** Tiranë
**Independence from the Ottoman Empire:** November 28, 1912
**What it means:** The double-headed black eagle represents an incident when a native prince of the 15th century successfully raised his red-coloured flag bearing the eagle, in rebellion against the Turks.

## BELARUS

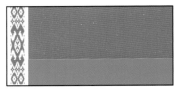

**Adopted:** 1995
**Ratio:** 1:2
**Capital:** Minsk
**Independence (from Soviet Union):** August 25, 1991
**What it means:** The red is thought to signify the blood shed by the patriots of Belarus. The red embroidered pattern is Belarusian national ornamentation.

## BOSNIA AND HERZEGOVINA

**Adopted:** February 1998
**Ratio:** 1:2
**Capital:** Sarajevo
**Independence from Yugoslavia; declared:** March 3, 1992
**What it means:** The three points of the yellow triangle are understood to stand for the three nations of Bosnia: Bosniaks, Croats and Serbs

## BULGARIA

**Adopted:** 1990
**Ratio:** 3:5
**Capital:** Sofia
**Independence (declared; from Ottoman Empire):** September 22, 1908
**What it means:** The white stands for peace, love and freedom; the green for the country's agricultural resources; and the red for the independence movement and the courage of the freedom fighters.

## CROATIA

**Adopted:** 1990
**Ratio:** 1:2
**Capital:** Zagreb
**Independence from Yugoslavia:** June 25, 1991
**What it means:** The stripes feature the traditional pan-Slavic colours. The national coat of arms in the middle has a main shield with five shields on top. The checkerboard design is an ancient symbol of the Croatian kings.

## ESTONIA

**Adopted:** 1990
**Ratio:** 7:11
**Capital:** Tallinn
**Independence (recognised; from Soviet Union):** August 20, 1991
**What it means:** The blue is a symbol of faith as well as the sky, seas and lakes; black of historic suppression as well as the soil; and white represents virtue, enlightenment and snow, as also for the country's freedom struggle.

## GREECE

**Adopted:** 1822
**Ratio:** 2:3
**Capital:** Athens
**Independence from the Ottoman Empire:** 1829
**What it means:** The nine stripes are taken for the nine syllables in the battle cry for independence, translated as "Freedom or death". The cross symbolises Greek religious faith.

Tallinn
ESTONIA
Riga LATVIA
Moscow
LITHUANIA
Vilniusa
Minsk
BELARUS
Kiev
UKRAINE
MOLDOVA
Budapest
Chisinau
HUNGARY ROMANIA
CROATIA — Zagreb
Bucharest
SERBIA
Belgrade
BOSNIA AND
HERZEGOVINA Sarajevo
BULGARIA
Sofia
MONTENEGRO
Capital: Podgorica
Tiranë Skopje
ALBANIA
KOSOVO
Capital: Pristina
GREECE
MACEDONIA
Athens

**RUSSIA**

### KOSOVO

**Adopted:** February 17, 2008
**Ratio:** 2:3
**Capital:** Pristina
**Independence (from Serbia, declared):** February 2008
**What it means:** The six stars represent Kosovo's six major ethnic groups: Albanians, Serbs, Turks, Gorani, Roma and Bosniaks. The blue background is designed to be neutral.

### HUNGARY

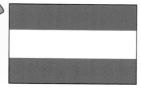

**Adopted on:** October 1, 1957
**Ratio:** 2:3
**Capital:** Budapest
**Independence (unification by King Stephen I):** 1001
**What it means:** Designed after the French tricolour. The red stands for strength, green for hope, and white for faithfulness.

### LATVIA

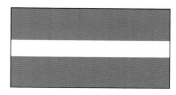

**Adopted:** 1900
**Ratio:** 1:2
**Capital:** Riga
**Independence (recognised; from Soviet Union):** August 21, 1991
**What it means:** The flag represents a legend about a Latvian tribal leader who was wrapped in a white cloth after he was injured in a battle. A part of the cloth became stained with his blood, while the rest remained white.

### LITHUANIA

**Adopted:** 1989
**Ratio:** 3:5
**Capital:** Vilnius
**Independence (recognised; from Soviet Union):** September 6, 1991
**What it means:** The yellow symbolises ripening wheat and freedom from want or need; green signifies hope and also represents the country's forests; and red stands for patriotism and right to freedom.

### MACEDONIA

**Adopted on:** October 5, 1995
**Ratio:** 1:2
**Capital:** Skopje
**Independence from Yugoslavia:** September 8, 1991
**What it means:** The design of the 'golden sun' finds mention in the country's national anthem. Red is a traditional colour of Macedonia.

### MOLDOVA

**Adopted:** 1990
**Ratio:** 1:2
**Capital:** Chisinau
**Independence (from Soviet Union):** August 27, 1991
**What it means:** The flag reflects the tricolour of Romania, of which Moldova was once a part. The emblem is a Roman eagle carrying a yellow cross in its beak, a green olive branch and a yellow sceptre in its talons.

### MONTENEGRO

**Adopted:** July 13, 2004
**Ratio:** 1:2
**Capital:** Podgorica
**Independence (from Serbia):** May 2006
**What it means:** The flag carries the state coat of arms of a double-headed golden eagle, which was established during the time of Prince Danilo Petrović Njegoš, the founder of the modern State of Montenegrin.

### ROMANIA

**Adopted:** 1989
**Ratio:** 2:3
**Capital:** Bucharest
**Independence from Turkey:** May 9, 1877
**What it means:** The tricolour goes back to Romania's past association with Moldova and Wallachia. The flag came into existence when Moldova and Wallachia united to form Romania, though that flag had horizontal stripes.

### RUSSIA

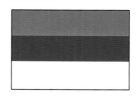

**Adopted:** 1991
**Ratio:** 2:3
**Capital:** Moscow
**Independence (from Soviet Union):** August 24, 1991
**What it means:** The white represents nobility, blue, truthfulness and commitment and red, valour and love. The flag was adopted by the Russian Czar, Peter the Great, who was impressed by the Dutch tricolour.

### SERBIA

**Adopted:** August 16, 2004
**Ratio:** 2:3
**Capital:** Belgrade
**Independence (proclaimed after Montenegro voted for independence):** June 5, 2006
**What it means:** The Pan-Slavic colours red, blue and white stand for unity and independence, as well as freedom and revolutionary ideals.

### UKRAINE

**Adopted:** 1991
**Ratio:** 2:3
**Capital:** Kiev (Kyyiv)
**Independence (from Soviet Union):** August 24, 1991
**What it means:** The colours were said by Ukranian nationalists to symbolise blue skies over golden wheat fields of the Steppes plains and this has become de facto.

# THE MIDDLE EAST

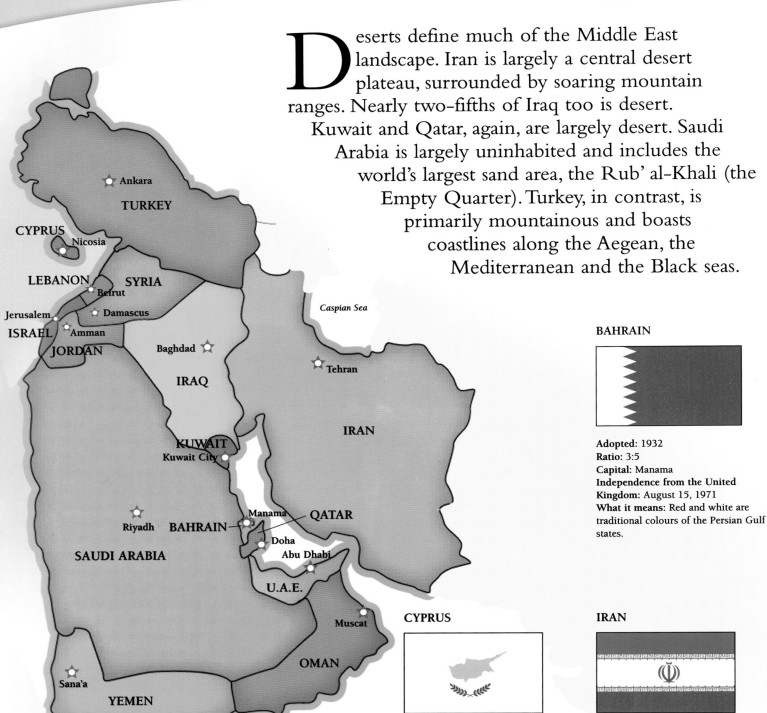

Deserts define much of the Middle East landscape. Iran is largely a central desert plateau, surrounded by soaring mountain ranges. Nearly two-fifths of Iraq too is desert. Kuwait and Qatar, again, are largely desert. Saudi Arabia is largely uninhabited and includes the world's largest sand area, the Rub' al-Khali (the Empty Quarter). Turkey, in contrast, is primarily mountainous and boasts coastlines along the Aegean, the Mediterranean and the Black seas.

**BAHRAIN**

**Adopted:** 1932
**Ratio:** 3:5
**Capital:** Manama
**Independence from the United Kingdom:** August 15, 1971
**What it means:** Red and white are traditional colours of the Persian Gulf states.

**CYPRUS**

**Adopted:** 1960
**Ratio:** 3:5
**Capital:** Nicosia
**Independence from the United Kingdom:** August 16, 1960
**What it means:** The olive branches symbolise the hope for peace between the island's Greek and Turkish communities. The copper-coloured outline of the island's map is for its name, which is Greek for 'copper'.

**IRAN**

**Adopted:** 1980
**Ratio:** 4:7
**Capital:** Tehran
**Independence:** April 1, 1979
**What it means:** The Arabic phrase *Allahu Akbar* ('God is great') is repeated 22 times along the edges of the green and red bands. The coat of arms can be taken as a stylised Arabic representation of the word Allah.

## IRAQ

**Adopted:** 1991
**Ratio:** 1:2
**Capital:** Baghdad
**Independence from League of Nations mandate under British control:** October 3, 1932
**What it means:** The phrase *Allahu Akbar* is incorporated between the stars. Red, green, white and black are the traditional colours across the Arab world.

## ISRAEL

**Adopted:** 1948
**Ratio:** 8:11
**Capital:** Jerusalem
**Independence from League of Nations mandate under British control:** May 14, 1948
**What it means:** The six-pointed star is known as the Magen David (Star of David) and is supposed to symbolise King David's shield. Blue and white are taken from the traditional Jewish prayer shawl.

## JORDAN

**Adopted:** 1928
**Ratio:** 1:2
**Capital:** Amman
**Independence from League of Nations mandate under British control:** May 25, 1946
**What it means:** The hoist-side triangle is symbolic of the Great Arab Revolt of 1916. The seven-pointed star signifies the opening seven verses of the Qur'an.

## KUWAIT

**Adopted:** 1961
**Ratio:** 1:2
**Capital:** Kuwait City
**Independence from the United Kingdom:** June 19, 1961
**What it means:** Green stands for the fertile land, white for purity, red for the blood of the enemy, and black for the enemy's defeat.

## LEBANON

**Adopted:** 1943
**Ratio:** 2:3
**Capital:** Beirut
**Independence from League of Nations mandate under French control:** November 22, 1943
**What it means:** The cedar tree has traditionally been a symbol for immortality, strength and wealth.

## OMAN

**Adopted:** 1995
**Ratio:** Usually 1:2
**Capital:** Muscat
**Independence (the Portuguese were driven out):** 1650
**What it means:** The coat of arms is a dagger in its sheath superimposed on two crossed swords in their holders.

## QATAR

**Adopted:** 1949
**Ratio:** 11:28
**Capital:** Doha (Ad-Dawhah)
**Independence from the United Kingdom:** September 3, 1971
**What it means:** It is said that the original red dye on the flag got altered into maroon in the Qatar sun! The flag looks similar to that of Bahrain, since Qatar was once a part of Bahrain.

## SAUDI ARABIA

**Adopted:** 1973
**Ratio:** 2:3
**Capital:** Riyadh
**Independence (unification of the kingdom):** September 23, 1932
**What it means:** Green is a traditional colour in Islamic flags. The Arabic inscription reads: "There is no god but Allah; Muhammad is the prophet of God."

## SYRIA

**Adopted:** 1980
**Ratio:** 2:3
**Capital:** Damascus
**Independence from League of Nations mandate under French control:** April 17, 1946
**What it means:** The stars represent Syria and Egypt, which were briefly united in 1958 to form the United Arab Republic. The colours are based on the Arab Liberation Flag.

## TURKEY

**Adopted:** 1936
**Ratio:** Approximately 2:3
**Capital:** Ankara
**Independence (republic declared):** October 29, 1923
**What it means:** The crescent and the star are symbols of Islam.

## UNITED ARAB EMIRATES

**Adopted:** 1971
**Ratio:** 1:2
**Capital:** Abu Dhabi
**Independence from the United Kingdom:** December 2, 1971
**What it means:** Incorporates the traditional Arab colours of unity and nationalism.

## YEMEN

**Adopted:** 1990
**Ratio:** 2:3
**Capital:** Sana'a
**Independence (republic declared with the union of North Yemen and South Yemen):** May 22, 1990
**What it means:** The flag was adopted upon the unification of North and South Yemen.

# WESTERN AND SOUTHERN
# ASIA

Afghanistan, Armenia, Bhutan and Nepal in, Western Asia, are landlocked countries. Rugged mountains make for some of the world's most difficult terrain in the rest of this region.

**AZERBAIJAN**

**GEORGIA**

T'bilisi

Yerevan

Baku

*Caspian Sea*

**ARMENIA**

Astana

**KAZAKHSTAN**

**UZBEKISTAN**

Ashgabat

Tashkent

Bishkek

**KYRGYZSTAN**

**TURKMENISTAN**

Dushanbe

**TAJIKISTAN**

Kabul

**AFGHANISTAN**

Islamabad

**PAKISTAN**

**NEPAL**

Kathmandu

**BHUTAN**

Thimphu

Dhaka

New Delhi

**INDIA**

**BANGLADESH**

**MALDIVES**

Colombo

Male

**SRI LANKA**

## AFGHANISTAN

**Adopted:** 2002
**Ratio:** 1:2
**Capital:** Kabul
**Independence (from U.K. control over foreign affairs):** August 19, 1919
**What it means:** The coat of arms found in the centre of the flag incorporates a mosque encircled by sheaves of wheat and an Islamic inscription.

## ARMENIA

**Adopted:** 1990
**Ratio:** 1:2
**Capital:** Yerevan
**Independence (from Soviet Union):** September 21, 1991
**What it means:** Red is said to be symbolic of the blood shed by Armenians in their freedom struggle; blue of their skies and hope; and orange of hard work.

## AZERBAIJAN

**Adopted:** 1991
**Ratio:** 1:2
**Capital:** Baku
**Independence (from Soviet Union):** August 30, 1991
**What it means:** The crescent and the star are symbols of Islam. The eight-pointed stars are thought to represent the eight traditional Turkic peoples.

## BANGLADESH

**Adopted:** 1972
**Ratio:** 6:10
**Capital:** Dhaka
**Independence (from Pakistan):** March 26, 1971
**What it means:** The disc symbolises the 'rising sun of a new country,' and the colour red symbolises the blood that was shed in the struggle for independence.

## BHUTAN

**Adopted:** 1969
**Ratio:** 2:3
**Capital:** Thimphu
**Independence from India:** August 8, 1949
**What it means:** The 'thunder' dragon at the centre is the country's national emblem. White is a symbol of purity and loyalty, yellow of the king's power and orange of Buddhist religious practices and monastries.

## GEORGIA

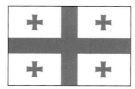

**Adopted:** 2004
**Ratio:** 2:3
**Capital:** T'bilisi
**Independence from Soviet Union:** April 9, 1991
**What it means:** The central cross connects all four sides of the flag, with each corner featuring the bolnur-katskhuri crosses. The five-cross theme dates back to the 14th century.

## INDIA

**Adopted:** 1947
**Ratio:** 2:3
**Capital:** New Delhi
**Independence (from the United Kingdom):** August 15, 1947
**What it means:** The orange (courage and sacrifice), white (peace and truth) and green (faith and chivalry) flag features a 24-spoked Buddhist charka ('Wheel of the Law') at the centre. This wheel stands for non-violence.

## KAZAKHSTAN

**Adopted:** June 4, 1992
**Ratio:** Approximately 1:2
**Capital:** Astana
**Independence from the Soviet Union:** December 16, 1991
**What it means:** Traditional Kazakh ornamentation is featured on the hoist side. A golden steppe eagle in flight is depicted below the shining sun.

## KYRGYZSTAN

**Adopted on:** March 3, 1992
**Ratio:** Approximately 3:5
**Capital:** Bishkek
**Independence from the Soviet Union:** August 31, 1991
**What it means:** The red background is said to have been adopted from the flag carried by the famed Kyrgyz hero, Manas the Noble. The 40 rays of the sun are symbolic of the tribes that the leader helped unite to form the nation.

## MALDIVES

**Adopted:** 1965
**Ratio:** 2:3
**Capital:** Male
**Independence (from the United Kingdom):** July 26, 1965
**What it means:** Red was the colour of the country's first flag. The green panel with a crescent is symbolic of Islam.

## NEPAL

**Adopted:** 1962
**Ratio:** 4:3
**Capital:** Kathmandu
**Independence (unified by Prithvi Narayan Shah):** 1768
**What it means:** Two triangles overlap, one with a crescent moon and the other bearing a 12-pointed sun. Red is the colour of the national flower, the rhododendron. The blue stands for peace.

## PAKISTAN

**Adopted:** 1947
**Ratio:** 2:3
**Capital:** Islamabad
**Independence (from the United Kingdom):** August 14, 1947
**What it means:** The traditional symbols of Islam are used. The white represents the country's non-Muslim population. The star is symbolic of knowledge and light, and the crescent, of progress.

## SRI LANKA

**Adopted:** 1978
**Ratio:** 1:2
**Capital:** Colombo
**Independence (from the United Kingdom):** February 4, 1948
**What it means:** The dark-red rectangle has a lion holding a sword, and four bo leaves, associated with Buddhism, at the corners. The thinner green and orange panels represent the minority Islamic and Tamil communities.

## TAJIKISTAN

**Adopted on:** November 24, 1992
**Ratio:** 1:2
**Capital:** Dushanbe
**Independence from Soviet Union:** September 9, 1991
**What it means:** The centred crown and the arc of seven gold stars are said to symbolise unity among the country's various social classes.

## TURKMENISTAN

**Adopted on:** February 19, 1997
**Ratio:** 1:2
**Capital:** Ashgabat
**Independence from the Soviet Union:** October 27, 1991
**What it means:** The five carpet motifs on the hoist-side are representative of the country's rich, traditional carpet industry.

## UZBEKISTAN

**Adopted on:** November 18, 1991
**Ratio:** Approximately 1:2
**Capital:** Tashkent
**Independence from the Soviet Union:** September 1, 1991
**What it means:** The 12 stars are for the 12 months in the year as well as for the constellations in the zodiac.

# EAST AND SOUTHEAST ASIA

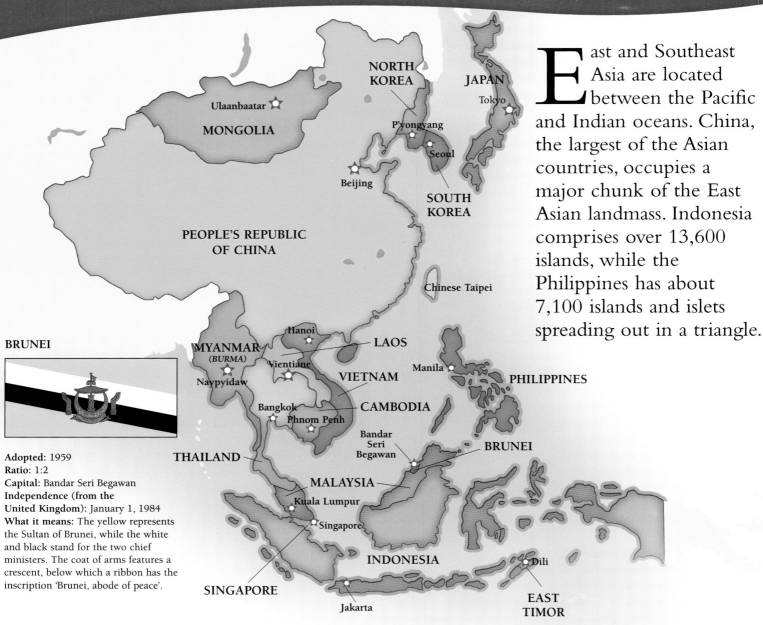

**NORTH KOREA**

**JAPAN**
Tokyo

Ulaanbaatar
**MONGOLIA**

P'yongyang
Seoul

Beijing

**SOUTH KOREA**

**PEOPLE'S REPUBLIC OF CHINA**

Chinese Taipei

Hanoi

**MYANMAR (BURMA)**
**LAOS**
Vientiane
Naypyidaw
**VIETNAM**
Manila
**PHILIPPINES**

Bangkok
**CAMBODIA**
Phnom Penh

Bandar Seri Begawan

**BRUNEI**

**THAILAND**

**MALAYSIA**
Kuala Lumpur

Singapore

**INDONESIA**
Dili

**SINGAPORE**

Jakarta

**EAST TIMOR**

East and Southeast Asia are located between the Pacific and Indian oceans. China, the largest of the Asian countries, occupies a major chunk of the East Asian landmass. Indonesia comprises over 13,600 islands, while the Philippines has about 7,100 islands and islets spreading out in a triangle.

## BRUNEI

**Adopted:** 1959
**Ratio:** 1:2
**Capital:** Bandar Seri Begawan
**Independence (from the United Kingdom):** January 1, 1984
**What it means:** The yellow represents the Sultan of Brunei, while the white and black stand for the two chief ministers. The coat of arms features a crescent, below which a ribbon has the inscription 'Brunei, abode of peace'.

## CAMBODIA

**Adopted:** 1993
**Ratio:** 2:3
**Capital:** Phnom Penh
**Independence from France:** November 9, 1953
**What it means:** Red and blue are the country's traditional colours. At the centre is the three-towered temple complex of Angkor Wat, making it the only national flag to feature a building.

## PEOPLE'S REPUBLIC OF CHINA

**Adopted:** 1949
**Ratio:** 2:3
**Capital:** Beijing
**Independence (People's Republic established):** October 1, 1949
**What it means:** Red, besides being the Chinese traditional colour, represents the communist revolution. The large star stands for the Chinese Communist Party, with the other four smaller ones denoting the four social classes.

## EAST TIMOR

**Adopted:** 2002
**Ratio:** 1:2
**Capital:** Dili
**Independence (recognised; from Portugal):** May 20, 2002
**What it means:** The colour yellow represents centuries of colonial repression, black stands for uncertainities that need to be overcome and red is for freedom struggle. The white star is the 'light that guides'.

## INDONESIA

**Adopted:** 1945
**Ratio:** 2:3
**Capital:** Jakarta
**Independence (declared; from the Netherlands):** August 17, 1945
**What it means:** The flag goes back to the 13th century, when the Majapahit Empire used a similar flag. Indonesians consider the traditional colours of red (courage) and white (honesty) holy.

## JAPAN

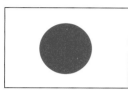

**Adopted:** 1870
**Ratio:** 2:3
**Capital:** Tokyo
**Independence (traditional founding):** 660 BC
**What it means:** The red disc of the sun (Hinomaru) is a traditional Japanese symbol. The white stands for honesty and purity.

## KOREA, NORTH

**Adopted:** 1948
**Ratio:** 1:2
**Capital:** P'yongyang
**Independence (from Japan):** August 15, 1945
**What it means:** The red stripe and the star represent the communist ideology. The blue and white stripes, respectively, symbolise peace and purity.

## KOREA, SOUTH

**Adopted:** 1950
**Ratio:** 2:3
**Capital:** Seoul
**Independence (from Japan):** August 15, 1945
**What it means:** The flag is called *Taegukki*. The yin-yang symbol stands for unity. The four sets of black bars represent sun, moon, earth and heaven.

## LAOS

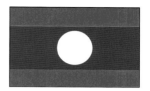

**Adopted:** 1975
**Ratio:** 2:3
**Capital:** Vientiane
**Independence (from France):** July 19, 1949
**What it means:** The white disc on a blue field is believed to be symbolic of the moon glowing over the Mekong River.

## MALAYSIA

**Adopted:** 1963
**Ratio:** 1:2
**Capital:** Kuala Lumpur
**Independence (from the United Kingdom):** August 31, 1957
**What it means:** The 14 stripes and 14 points of the star represent the original 14 states of Malaysia. Since Singapore left the federation in 1965, the 14th stripe and point is said to represent the Malaysian government.

## MONGOLIA

**Adopted:** 1940
**Ratio:** 1:2
**Capital:** Ulaanbaatar
**Independence (from China):** July 11, 1921
**What it means:** The sky blue is Mongolia's national colour. The traditional emblem of *soyonbo* is featured in the red bar on the hoist side.

## MYANMAR (BURMA)

**Adopted:** 1974
**Ratio:** 5:9
**Capital:** Naypyidaw (as of 2005)
**Independence (from the United Kingdom):** January 4, 1948
**What it means:** The 14 stars are for the 14 states and other divisions of the country. These encircle a cogwheel framing a stalk of rice, a symbol of the peasant force and the union of industry and agriculture.

## PHILIPPINES, THE

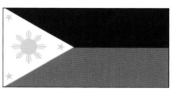

**Adopted:** 1898
**Ratio:** Usually 1:2
**Capital:** Manila
**Independence (from Spain):** June 12, 1898
**What it means:** The three stars are for Luzon, Mindanao and Visayan. The sun symbolises independence, and its eight rays, the provinces that rose against the Spanish rule. Blue and red stand for patriotism and courage.

## SINGAPORE

**Adopted:** 1959
**Ratio:** 2:3
**Capital:** Singapore
**Independence (from Malaysian Federation):** August 9, 1965
**What it means:** The white crescent is symbolic of the young nation. The five stars stand for democracy, peace, progress, justice and equality. Red signifies universal brotherhood and white, purity and virtue.

## THAILAND

**Adopted:** 1917
**Ratio:** 2:3
**Capital:** Bangkok
**Independence (traditional founding):** 1238
**What it means:** The common symbolisms are – red for the blood sacrificed by the people for their country, white for the purity of Buddhism, and blue for the monarchy.

## VIETNAM

**Adopted:** 1955
**Ratio:** 2:3
**Capital:** Hanoi
**Independence (from France):** September 2, 1945
**What it means:** The main classes of workers are represented by the five points of the star.

# WEST AFRICA

West Africa is the westernmost region of the African continent. The northwestern region – comprised of Morocco (including Western Sahara), Algeria, Tunisia (and sometimes Lybia) – is known as the Maghreb, from an Arabic word meaning "western". West Africa incorporates a great span of cultures, geography and bioregions. A large area of west Africa is dominated by the Sahara desert, which spreads through nearly all of northern Africa.

### ALGERIA

**Adopted:** 1962
**Ratio:** 2:3
**Capital:** Algiers
**Independence (from France):** July 5, 1962
**What it means:** The colour green, and the crescent and star are Islamic symbols.

### BENIN

**Adopted:** 1959
**Ratio:** 2:3
**Capital:** Porto-Novo
**Independence (from France):** August 1, 1960
**What it means:** Features pan-African colours, symbolic of African unity.

### BURKINA FASO

**Adopted:** 1984
**Ratio:** Approximately 2:3
**Capital:** Ouagadougou
**Independence (from France):** August 5, 1960
**What it means:** The red is symbolic of the 1984 revolution.

### CAMEROON

**Adopted:** 1975
**Ratio:** Approximately 2:3
**Capital:** Yaoundé
**Independence (from UN trusteeship):** January 1, 1960
**What it means:** The central star symbolises national unity.

### CAPE VERDE

**Adopted:** 1992
**Ratio:** 3:5
**Capital:** Praia
**Independence (from Portugal):** July 5, 1975
**What it means:** The blue field and the stars represent the 10 main islands.

### CÔTE D'IVOIRE (IVORY COAST)

**Adopted:** 1959
**Ratio:** Approximately 2:3
**Capital:** Yamoussoukro
**Independence (from France):** August 7, 1960
**What it means:** The flag symbolises dynamic growth, peace and hope.

### EQUATORIAL GUINEA

**Adopted:** 1979
**Ratio:** Approximately 2:3
**Capital:** Malabo
**Independence (from Spain):** October 12, 1968
**What it means:** The six stars represent the five principal islands and the mainland.

### GABON

**Adopted:** 1960
**Ratio:** 3:4
**Capital:** Libreville
**Independence (from France):** August 17, 1960
**What it means:** The green and yellow signify the country's natural wealth, while the blue represents the coast.

### GAMBIA

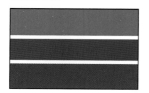

**Adopted:** 1965
**Ratio:** 2:3
**Capital:** Banjul
**Independence (from the United Kingdom):** February 18, 1965
**What it means:** Red, blue and green represent Gambia's natural reserves.

### GHANA

**Adopted:** 1957
**Ratio:** 2:3
**Capital:** Accra
**Independence (from the United Kingdom):** March 6, 1957
**What it means:** The black star stands for 'African freedom'.

### GUINEA

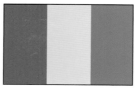

**Adopted:** 1958
**Ratio:** 2:3
**Capital:** Conakry
**Independence (from France):** October 2, 1958
**What it means:** The flag incorporates pan-African colours.

### GUINEA-BISSAU

**Adopted:** 1973
**Ratio:** Approximately 1:2
**Capital:** Bissau
**Independence (declared; from Portugal):** September 24, 1973
**What it means:** The black star stands for the people's right to freedom.

## LIBERIA

**Adopted:** 1847
**Ratio:** 10:19
**Capital:** Monrovia
**Independence:** July 26, 1847
**What it means:** The stripes are for the men who signed the Liberian Declaration of Independence.

## MALI

**Adopted:** 1961
**Ratio:** 2:3
**Capital:** Bamako
**Independence (from France):** September 22, 1960
**What it means:** The Mali flag uses pan-African colours.

## MAURITANIA

**Adopted:** 1959
**Ratio:** 2:3
**Capital:** Nouakchott
**Independence (from France):** November 28, 1960
**What it means:** The green field, the star and the crescent represent Islam.

## MOROCCO

**Adopted:** 1915
**Ratio:** 2:3
**Capital:** Rabat
**Independence (from France):** March 2, 1956
**What it means:** Red is for the descendants of Prophet Muhammad.

## NIGER

**Adopted:** 1959
**Ratio:** Approximately 6:7
**Capital:** Niamey
**Independence (from France):** August 3, 1960
**What it means:** The orange disc symbolises the sun.

## NIGERIA

**Adopted:** 1960
**Ratio:** 1:2
**Capital:** Abuja
**Independence (from the United Kingdom):** October 1, 1960
**What it means:** White reminds of peace and unity, and green of the fertile land.

## SÃO TOMÉ AND PRÍNCIPE

**Adopted:** 1975
**Ratio:** 1:2
**Capital:** São Tomé
**Independence (from Portugal):** July 12, 1975
**What it means:** The red triangle is a symbol for the freedom struggle.

## SENEGAL

**Adopted:** 1960
**Ratio:** Approximately 2:3
**Capital:** Dakar
**Independence (from France):** April 4, 1960
**What it means:** The green star is symbolic of hope and unity.

## SIERRA LEONE

**Adopted:** 1961
**Ratio:** 2:3
**Capital:** Freetown
**Independence (from the United Kingdom):** April 27, 1961
**What it means:** Green stands for agricultural, white for unity and justice, and blue for the natural harbour at Freetown.

## TOGO

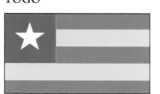

**Adopted:** 1960
**Ratio:** Approximately 3:5
**Capital:** Lomé
**Independence (from French-administered UN trusteeship):** April 27, 1960
**What it means:** The red field represents the values of love, loyalty and charity. It features the 'Star of Hope' and emphasises purity and national unity.

## TUNISIA

**Adopted:** 1835
**Ratio:** 2:3
**Capital:** Tunis
**Independence (from France):** March 20, 1956
**What it means:** The crescent and star are traditional symbols of Islam.

WESTERN SAHARA (DISPUTED)

TUNISIA — Tunis, Algiers
MOROCCO — Rabat
ALGERIA
BURKINA FASO
MAURITANIA — Nouakchott
MALI — Bamako
NIGER — Niamey
CAPE VERDE — Praia
SENEGAL — Dakar
GAMBIA — Banjul
GUINEA-BISSAU — Bissau
GUINEA — Conakry
SIERRA LEONE — Freetown
LIBERIA — Monrovia
IVORY COAST — Yamoussoukro
GHANA — Accra
TOGO — Lomé
BENIN — Porto-Novo
Ouagadougou
NIGERIA — Abuja
CAMEROON — Yaoundé
EQUATORIAL GUINEA — Malabo
SÃO TOMÉ AND PRÍNCIPE — São Tomé
GABON — Libreville

# EAST AFRICA

The Great Rift Valley is a vast geological feature stretching from Ethiopia to Mozambique in East Africa. About 160 kilometres (100 miles) east of the East African Rift System (of which the Great Rift Valley is a branch) is Kilimanjaro, which, at 5,895 metres (19,340 feet), is the highest point in Africa.

**Tripoli**

**LIBYA**

**Cairo**

**EGYPT**

**CHAD**

**N'Djamena**

**SUDAN**

**Khartoum**

**ERITREA**

**Asmara**

**DJIBOUTI**

**Djibouti**

**SOMALIA**

**Addis Ababa**

**ETHIOPIA**

**CENTRAL AFRICAN REPUBLIC**

**Bangui**

**UGANDA**

**Kampala**

**KENYA**

**Nairobi**

**Mogadishu**

**REPUBLIC OF THE CONGO**

**Brazzaville**

**DEMOCRATIC REPUBLIC OF THE CONGO**

**Kinshasa**

**RWANDA**

**Kigali**

**BURUNDI**

**Bujumbura**

**Victoria**

**SEYCHELLES**

## BURUNDI

**Adopted:** 1967
**Ratio:** 3:5
**Capital:** Bujumbura
**Independence (from UN trusteeship under Belgian administration):** July 1, 1962
**What it means:** The three stars represent the three main ethnic groups of the country – the Hutu, Tutsi and Twa.

## CENTRAL AFRICAN REPUBLIC

**Adopted:** 1958
**Ratio:** Approximately 3:5
**Capital:** Bangui
**Independence (from the United Kingdom):** August 13, 1960
**What it means:** The red stripe symbolises the bond between Africans and Europeans. The yellow star expresses hope for a bright future.

## CHAD

**Adopted:** 1959
**Ratio:** 2:3
**Capital:** N'Djamena
**Independence (from France):** August 11, 1960
**What it means:** Uses the pan-African colours of red and yellow with the French tricolour's blue and red.

## DEMOCRATIC REPUBLIC OF THE CONGO (ZAIRE)

**Adopted:** 1997
**Ratio:** 2:3
**Capital:** Kinshasa
**Independence (from France):** June 30, 1960
**What it means:** The six stars along the hoist were incorporated to represent the original provinces of Congo.

## DJIBOUTI

**Adopted:** 1977
**Ratio:** Not specified
**Capital:** Djibouti
**Independence (from France):** June 27, 1977
**What it means:** Blue represents the Issa people, and green the Afar people. The white triangle bears a red star for national unity.

## EGYPT

**Adopted:** 1984
**Ratio:** 2:3
**Capital:** Cairo
**Independence (from the United Kingdom):** February 28, 1922
**What it means:** Pan-African colours are used. The coat of arms is the golden eagle of the 12th-century ruler Saladin, who fought in the Crusades.

## ERITREA

**Adopted:** 1995
**Ratio:** 1:2
**Capital:** Asmara
**Independence (from Ethiopia):** May 24, 1993
**What it means:** The green, blue and red are the party colours of the Eritrean People's Liberation Front (EPLF), who had led the independence struggle. The olive branch circled by a wreath was inspired by the flag of the United Nations and signify the country's autonomy.

## ETHIOPIA

**Adopted:** 1996
**Ratio:** 1:2
**Capital:** Addis Ababa
**Independence :**
**What it means:** The green, gold and red of the flag of Ethiopia (the oldest independent state in Africa) were so often adopted by emerging independent African states that they became known as the Pan-African colours. The star stands for unity among the Ethiopian nationalities.

## KENYA

**Adopted:** 1963
**Ratio:** 2:3
**Capital:** Nairobi
**Independence (from the United Kingdom):** December 12, 1963
**What it means:** Black, red and green belonged to the Kenya African Union (KAU) party. White was added to represent the democractic party and national unity. The Masai shield and two crossed spears stand for national pride and tradition.

## LIBYA

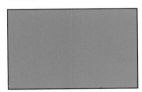

**Adopted:** 1977
**Ratio:** 1:2
**Capital:** Tripoli
**Independence (from Italy):** December 24, 1951
**What it means:** The only national flag to use a single colour.

## REPUBLIC OF THE CONGO

**Adopted:** 1958
**Ratio:** 2:3
**Capital:** Brazzaville
**Independence (from France):** August 15, 1960
**What it means:** Uses the pan-African colours which symbolise African independence and unity.

## RWANDA

**Adopted:** 2001
**Ratio:** Approximately 2:3
**Capital:** Kigali
**Independence (from Belgium-administered UN trusteeship):** July 1, 1962
**What it means:** Blue bears the message of happiness and peace. Yellow stands for economic progress, while green is symbolic of prosperity.

## SEYCHELLES

**Adopted:** 1996
**Ratio:** 1:2
**Capital:** Victoria
**Independence (from the United Kingdom):** June 29, 1976
**What it means:** The red, white and green are the colors of the Seychelles People's United Party (SPUP). The blue and yellow are of the Democratic Party.

## SOMALIA

**Adopted:** 1954
**Ratio:** 2:3
**Capital:** Mogadishu
**Independence (from the United Kingdom and Italy):** July 1, 1960
**What it means:** The blue field is inspired by the United Nations (UN) flag. The 'Star of Unity' is symbolic of the Somali people scattered across places such as Djibouti, Ethiopia and Kenya.

## SUDAN

**Adopted:** 1970
**Ratio:** 1:2
**Capital:** Khartoum
**Independence (from Egypt and the United Kingdom):** January 1, 1956
**What it means:** Red stands for socialism and progress, and white for peace and hope. Black recalls the name of the country (*sudan* is Arabic for 'black').

## UGANDA

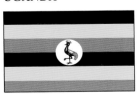

**Adopted:** 1962
**Ratio:** 2:3
**Capital:** Kampala
**Independence (from the United Kingdom):** October 9, 1962
**What it means:** The striped colours are from the tricolour of the Uganda People's Congress (UPC). The crested crane is the national symbol.

# CENTRAL AND SOUTHERN
# AFRICA

Central Africa lies across the Equator. The terrain consists of wide plateaus, which may reach a height of about 914 metres (3,000 feet) near the Angolan border. Central Africa's highest point is Margherita Peak – at 5,119 metres (16,795 feet). It is located on the eastern fringe of the Rift Valley.

Southern Africa too features a high interior plateau that consists of rolling grasslands. However, the monotony of the plateau is broken by the Kalahari desert and the Great Escarpment, a series of mountain ranges that run parallel to a narrow coastal strip. The Zambezi and the Limpopo are the largest rivers in the region.

## ANGOLA

**Adopted:** 1975
**Ratio:** 2:3
**Capital:** Luanda
**Independence (from Portugal):** November 11, 1975
**What it means:** The machete and the cogwheel in the central yellow emblem stand for agriculture and industry, while the star is symbolic of progress. The red colour represents the blood shed during the freedom struggle and the black stands for Africa.

## BOTSWANA

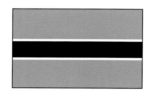

**Adopted:** 1966
**Ratio:** 2:3
**Capital:** Gaborone
**Independence (from the United Kingdom):** September 30, 1966
**What it means:** The blue background is symbolic of water and life, and the black-and-white centre, inspired by the coat of the national animal, zebra, signifies racial equality among the people.

## COMOROS

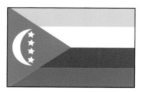

**Adopted:** 2001 (current flag)
**Ratio:** 2:3
**Capital:** Moroni
**Independence (from France):** July 6, 1975
**What it means:** The crescent and stars are Islamic symbols. The four stars represent the main islands of the union.

## LESOTHO

**Adopted:** 1987
**Ratio:** 9:14
**Capital:** Maseru
**Independence (from the United Kingdom):** October 4, 1966
**What it means:** The white triangle symbolises peace and features an outline of a shield with a spear and a traditional club. The green triangle stands for prosperity, while the blue band represents rain.

## MADAGASCAR

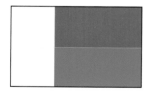

**Adopted:** 1958
**Ratio:** 2:3
**Capital:** Antananarivo
**Independence (from France):** June 26, 1960
**What it means:** Red and white are the traditional colours of Madagascar. Green is believed to recall the country's former peasant class (Hova).

## MALAWI

**Adopted:** 1964
**Ratio:** 2:3
**Capital:** Lilongwe
**Independence (from France):** July 6, 1964
**What it means:** Black (African heritage), red (blood of martyrs) and green (the land) are the colours of the Malawi Congress Party. The rising sun represents dawn of hope and freedom for the whole of Africa.

## MAURITIUS

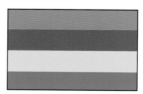

**Adopted:** 1968
**Ratio:** 2:3
**Capital:** Port Louis
**Independence (from the United Kingdom):** March 12, 1968
**What it means:** Red stands for the independence movement, blue for the Indian Ocean, yellow for the 'light of freedom shining over the island,' and green for the rich vegetation.

## MOZAMBIQUE

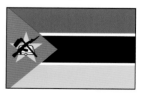

**Adopted:** 1983
**Ratio:** Approximately 2:3
**Capital:** Maputo
**Independence (from Portugal):** June 25, 1975
**What it means:** The yellow star bears an open book (education) overlaid by a hoe (peasantry) and rifle (defence of the land).

## SOUTH AFRICA

**Adopted:** 1994
**Ratio:** 2:3
**Capital:** Pretoria
**Independence (from the United Kingdom):** May 31, 1910; proclaimed a republic on May 31, 1961
**What it means:** The Y-shape symbolises 'converging of paths' and unification. The red, white and blue were taken from the colours of the 19th-century Boer Republics. The yellow, black and green are from the African National Congress (ANC) flag.

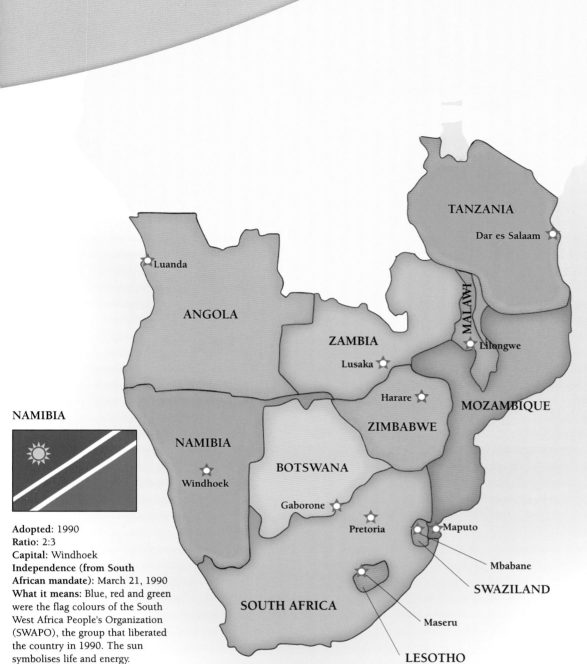

## NAMIBIA

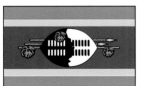

**Adopted:** 1990
**Ratio:** 2:3
**Capital:** Windhoek
**Independence (from South African mandate):** March 21, 1990
**What it means:** Blue, red and green were the flag colours of the South West Africa People's Organization (SWAPO), the group that liberated the country in 1990. The sun symbolises life and energy.

## SWAZILAND

**Adopted:** 1967
**Ratio:** 2:3
**Capital:** Mbabane
**Independence (from the United Kingdom):** September 6, 1968
**What it means:** The background is based on the flag that King Sobhuza II gave to the Swazi Pioneer Corps in 1941. The centered Swazi shield features two spears and a staff with hanging feather tassels of the widowbird.

## TANZANIA

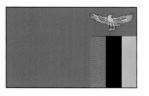

**Adopted:** 1964
**Ratio:** 2:3
**Capital:** Dar es Salaam
**Independence (republic formed by union of Tanganyika and Zanzibar):** April 26, 1964
**What it means:** The green and black were taken from the Tanganyika flag and represent the land and people of Tanzania. The blue, for the sea, came from the Zanzibar flag.

## ZAMBIA

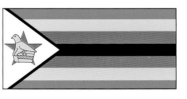

**Adopted:** 1964
**Ratio:** 2:3
**Capital:** Lusaka
**Independence (from the United Kingdom):** October 24, 1964
**What it means:** The colours belonged to the United Nationalist Independent Party, the main political party during the time Zambia became independent. The eagle, taken from the national coat of arms, is symbolic of freedom and patriotism.

## ZIMBABWE

**Adopted:** 1980
**Ratio:** 1:2
**Capital:** Harare
**Independence (from the United Kingdom):** April 18, 1980
**What it means:** The Zimbabwe Bird is a national emblem. The triangle stands for peace and the red star denotes the government's socialist ideals.

# OCEANIA

Oceania is the name for a group of islands distributed across the Pacific Ocean. It includes over 10,000 islands and is normally divided into the regions of Australasia (Australia and New Zealand), Melanesia, Micronesia and Polynesia. Australia is the world's smallest continent as well as the sixth largest country. An isolated island, New Zealand is separated from its nearest neighbour, Australia, by more than 1,600 km (1,000 miles).

## AUSTRALIA

**Adopted:** 1909
**Ratio:** 1:2
**Capital:** Canberra
**Independence (federation of U.K. colonies):** January 1, 1901
**What it means:** The Union Jack is featured on the upper hoist side, with the seven-pointed Commonwealth Star below. The five stars on the right half represent the Southern Cross constellation.

## FIJI ISLANDS

**Adopted:** 1970
**Ratio:** 1:2
**Capital:** Suva
**Independence (from the United Kingdom):** October 10, 1970
**What it means:** The blue field is symbolic of the Pacific Ocean. The coat of arms displays a golden British lion, with the panels displaying sugar cane, a palm tree, bananas and the dove of peace.

## KIRIBATI

**Adopted:** 1979
**Ratio:** 1:2
**Capital:** Bairiki
**Independence (from the United Kingdom):** July 12, 1979
**What it means:** The upper half shows a local frigate bird flying over the rising sun, as a symbol of strength and power at sea. The blue and white bands represent the Pacific Ocean.

## MARSHALL ISLANDS

**Adopted:** 1979
**Ratio:** 10:19
**Capital:** Dalap-Uliga-Darrit (on Majuro Atoll)
**Independence (from U.S.-administered UN trusteeship):** October 21, 1986
**What it means:** The orange and white signify the country's parallel island chains. The 24-pointed star stands for as many districts of the islands.

## MICRONESIA

**Adopted:** 1978
**Ratio:** 10:19
**Capital:** Palikir
**Independence (from U.S.-administered UN trusteeship):** November 3, 1986
**What it means:** The four stars stand for the four island groups in the country, centred on a blue field for the Pacific Ocean.

## NAURU

**Adopted:** 1968
**Ratio:** 1:2
**Capital:** No official capital
**Independence (from Australia-, New Zealand-, and U.K.-administered UN trusteeship):** January 31, 1968
**What it means:** The yellow line represents the Equator, and the 12-pointed star stands for the 12 original tribes of Nauru.

## NEW ZEALAND

**Adopted:** 1902
**Ratio:** 1:2
**Capital:** Wellington
**Independence (from the United Kingdom):** September 26, 1907
**What it means:** The stars represent the Southern Cross constellation.

## PALAU

**Adopted:** 1981
**Ratio:** 5:8
**Capital:** Koror
**Independence (from U.S.-administered UN trusteeship):** October 1, 1994
**What it means:** Palauans regard the full moon, represented by the disc, auspicious for agriculture.

## PAPUA NEW GUINEA

**Adopted:** 1971
**Ratio:** 3:4
**Capital:** Port Moresby
**Independence (from Australia-administered UN trusteeship):** September 16, 1975
**What it means:** The five stars stand for the Southern Cross, while the bird-of-paradise is a local symbol. Red and black are native colours.

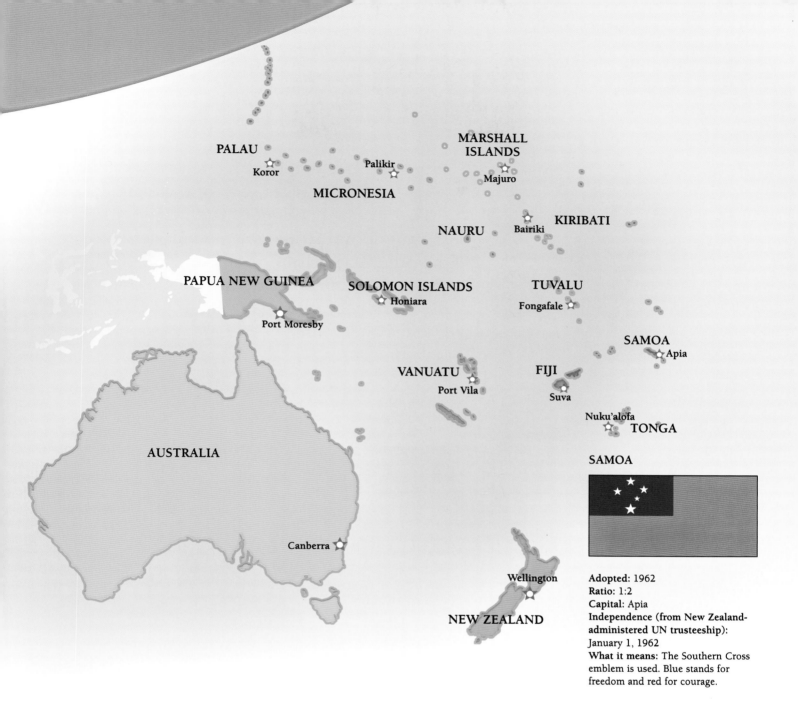

PALAU
Koror

Palikir
MICRONESIA

MARSHALL
ISLANDS
Majuro

NAURU Bairiki KIRIBATI

PAPUA NEW GUINEA

SOLOMON ISLANDS
Honiara

TUVALU
Fongafale

Port Moresby

VANUATU
Port Vila

FIJI
Suva

SAMOA
Apia

AUSTRALIA

Nuku'alofa
TONGA

SAMOA

Canberra

Wellington

NEW ZEALAND

**Adopted:** 1962
**Ratio:** 1:2
**Capital:** Apia
**Independence (from New Zealand-administered UN trusteeship):** January 1, 1962
**What it means:** The Southern Cross emblem is used. Blue stands for freedom and red for courage.

---

## SOLOMON ISLANDS

**Adopted:** 1977
**Ratio:** 1:2
**Capital:** Honiara
**Independence (from the United Kingdom):** July 7, 1978
**What it means:** The five white stars represent the country's original provinces. The blue triangle signifies water and the green, the land. The yellow stripe symbolises sunshine.

## TONGA

**Adopted:** 1875
**Ratio:** 1:2
**Capital:** Nuku'alofa
**Independence (from U.K. protectorate status):** June 4, 1970
**What it means:** The red field is symbolic of the blood shed by Jesus on the cross. The cross stands as a symbol of Christianity, with the white representing purity.

## TUVALU

**Adopted:** 1978
**Ratio:** 1:2
**Capital:** Fongafale (on Funafuti Atoll)
**Independence (from the United Kingdom):** October 1, 1978
**What it means:** The nine stars represent the nine islands that constitute the country.

## VANUATU

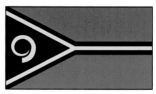

**Adopted:** 1990
**Ratio:** 3:5
**Capital:** Port Vila
**Independence (from France and the United Kingdom):** July 30, 1980
**What it means:** The Y-shape represents the shape formed by the islands.

# UNITED STATES OF AMERICA

T he United States is a federal republic made up of 50 states — 48 of these are connected in one continuous landmass. Alaska and Hawaii do not share their boundaries with any of the other states. Its total area of 9,529,063 sq km (3,679,192 square miles) makes the United States the world's fourth largest country (after Russia, Canada and China).

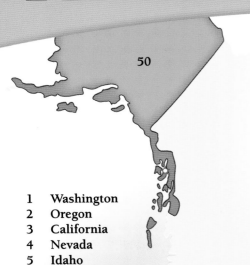

1   Washington
2   Oregon
3   California
4   Nevada
5   Idaho
6   Utah
7   Arizona
8   Montana
9   Wyoming
10  Colorado
11  New Mexico
12  North Dakota
13  South Dakota
14  Nebraska
15  Kansas
16  Oklahoma
17  Texas
18  Minnesota
19  Iowa
20  Missouri
21  Arkansas
22  Louisiana
23  Wisconsin
24  Illinois
25  Mississippi
26  Indiana
27  Kentucky
28  Tennessee
29  Alabama
30  Michigan

31  Ohio
32  Pennsylvania
33  West Virginia
34  Virginia
35  North Carolina
36  South Carolina
37  Georgia
38  Florida
39  New York
40  Vermont
41  New Hampshire
42  Maine
43  Massachusetts
44  Rhode Island
45  Connecticut
46  New Jersey
47  Delaware
48  Maryland
49  Hawaii
50  Alaska
*   District of Colombia

**Alabama**

Adopted: 1895
Ratio: can be square or rectangular
Capital: Montgomery
What it means: Based on the battle flag of the Confederate States during the Civil War.

**Alaska**

Adopted: 1959
Ratio: 2:3
Capital: Juneau
What it means: A 13-year-old boy, Benny Benson, designed this flag in 1926, depicting the North Star and the Ursa Major constellation.

**Arizona**

Adopted: 1913
Ratio: 2:3
Capital: Phoenix
What it means: The copper-coloured star represents the copper resources of Arizona.

**Arkansas**

Adopted: 1913
Ratio: 2:3
Capital: Little Rock
What it means: The diamond shape of the central white emblem symbolises the state's diamond production.

## California

**Adopted:** 1911
**Ratio:** 2:3
**Capital:** Sacramento
**What it means:** The flag bearing a grizzly bear goes back to an 1846 local revolt.

## Colorado

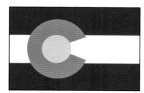

**Adopted:** 1911
**Ratio:** 2:3
**Capital:** Denver
**What it means:** The red 'C' recalls the Spanish word *colorado* ('red coloured'), from which the name of the state originated.

## Connecticut

**Adopted:** 1897
**Ratio:** 4:5
**Capital:** Hartford
**What it means:** The Latin inscription reads "He who transplanted still sustains us." This is based on a psalm.

## Delaware

**Adopted:** 1913
**Ratio:** 3:4
**Capital:** Dover
**What it means:** The date beneath the coat of arms is when Delaware became the first state to formally approve the U.S. Constitution.

## Florida

**Adopted:** 1900
**Ratio:** 2:3
**Capital:** Tallahassee
**What it means:** The flag recalls the Confederate flag of the Civil War. The state seal is at the centre.

## Georgia

**Adopted:** 2003
**Ratio:** 2:3
**Capital:** Atlanta
**What it means:** The 13 stars around the state's coat of arms refer to Georgia as one of the 13 original colonies.

## Hawaii

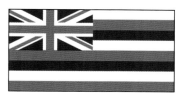

**Adopted:** 1845
**Ratio:** 1:2
**Capital:** Honolulu
**What it means:** The Union Jack can be traced to the year 1793, when a British army officer made a gift of the flag to the Hawaiian king.

## Idaho

**Adopted:** 1927
**Ratio:** 2:3
**Capital:** Boise
**What it means:** The flag is based on an earlier military banner.

## Illinois

**Adopted:** 1915
**Ratio:** 3:5
**Capital:** Sacramento
**What it means:** The dates 1818 and 1868, respectively, stand for statehood and the first time the state seal was used.

## Indiana

**Adopted:** 1917
**Ratio:** 2:3
**Capital:** Indianapolis
**What it means:** The 19 stars around the gold torch recall Indiana's status as the 19th state to join the Union.

## Iowa

**Adopted:** 1921
**Ratio:** 2:3
**Capital:** Des Moines
**What it means:** The flag recalls the French tricolour – Iowa was once a part of French Louisiana.

## Kansas

**Adopted:** 1925
**Ratio:** 3:5
**Capital:** Topeka
**What it means:** The sunflower was adopted as the state's floral emblem in 1903.

## Kentucky

**Adopted:** 1918
**Ratio:** 2:3
**Capital:** Frankfort
**What it means:** The theme of national unity is reflected in the state seal.

## Louisiana

**Adopted:** 1912
**Ratio:** 2:3
**Capital:** Baton Rouge
**What it means:** The pelican represents the spirit of self-sacrifice.

## Maine

**Adopted:** 1909
**Ratio:** 2:3
**Capital:** Augusta
**What it means:** The coat of arms depicts a farmer and a sailor representing the agricultural and shipbuilding industries. The Latin motto means, "I direct."

## Maryland

**Adopted:** 1904
**Ratio:** 2:3
**Capital:** Annapolis
**What it means:** The flag retains British heraldic symbols.

## Massachusetts

**Adopted:** 1908
**Ratio:** 2:3
**Capital:** Boston
**What it means:** The Latin motto reads "By the sword we seek peace, but peace only under liberty." The coat of arms on a white background served many Massachusetts regiments.

## Michigan

**Adopted:** 1911
**Ratio:** 2:3
**Capital:** Lansing
**What it means:** The state seal features the bald eagle, a shield, an elk and a moose. There are three Latin mottoes: "One out of many," "I will defend," and "If you seek a pleasant peninsula, look about you."

## Minnesota

**Adopted:** 1893
**Ratio:** 7:11
**Capital:** St Paul
**What it means:** The state's motto, 'Star of the north', is shown on the red ribbon. Minnesota was the northernmost state in the Union before Alaska joined it.

## Mississippi

**Adopted:** 1894
**Ratio:** 2:3
**Capital:** Jackson
**What it means:** The stripes retain the Stars and Bars of the Confederacy, while the canton features the Confederate Battle Flag.

## Missouri

**Adopted:** 1913
**Ratio:** 10:17
**Capital:** Jefferson City
**What it means:** The Latin motto reads: "The welfare of the people shall be the supreme law."

## Montana

**Adopted:** 1905
**Ratio:** 2:3
**Capital:** Helena
**What it means:** The state seal depicts the state's scenic landscape – the Rocky Mountains, the Great Falls, a river and forests. The plough, and the crossed pick and shovel are symbolic of agriculture and mining.

## Nebraska

**Adopted:** 1963
**Ratio:** 3:5
**Capital:** Lincoln
**What it means:** The 1867 state seal is themed around Nebraska's agricultural and industrial development.

## Nevada

**Adopted:** 1929
**Ratio:** 2:3
**Capital:** Carson City
**What it means:** The sagebrush is Nevada's state flower. The phrase 'Battle born' recalls Nevada's admission to the Union during the Civil War (1861-65).

## New Hampshire

**Adopted:** 1909
**Ratio:** 2:3
**Capital:** Concord
**What it means:** The state seal was adopted in 1784 and it features the frigate *Raleigh*, which was built in 1776 and was one of the first ships in the nation's navy.

## New Jersey

**Adopted:** 1896
**Ratio:** 2:3
**Capital:** Trenton
**What it means:** The field of buff (light tan) was taken from the uniform colour worn by New Jersey troops in the Revolutionary War (1775-83).

## New Mexico

**Adopted:** 1925
**Ratio:** 2:3
**Capital:** Santa Fe
**What it means:** The sun symbol belonged to the Zia Pueblo Indians. Yellow and red were inspired by the flag of Spain, which controlled New Mexico until the beginning of the 19th century.

## New York

**Adopted:** 1901
**Ratio:** 1:2
**Capital:** Albany
**What it means:** The coat of arms features a sun symbol and the two supporters of the shield – Liberty (on the left) and Justice.

## North Carolina

**Adopted:** 1885
**Ratio:** 2:3
**Capital:** Raleigh
**What it means:** May 20, 1775, recalls the first meeting of North Carolina citizens proclaiming their freedom from Great Britain.

## North Dakota

**Adopted:** 1911
**Ratio:** 2:3
**Capital:** Bismarck
**What it means:** The flag was earlier used by the state's military regiments.

## Ohio

**Adopted:** 1902
**Ratio:** 5:8
**Capital:** Columbus
**What it means:** The swallow-tailed shape of the flag was probably inspired by a standard carried by the U.S. cavalry during the Civil War.

## Oklahoma

**Adopted:** 1907
**Ratio:** 2:3
**Capital:** Oklahoma City
**What it means:** The bison-hide shield belongs to the Osage Indians. An olive branch and a Native American peace pipe are emblems of peace. The four small crosses are common motifs in Native American art and stand for high ideals.

## Oregon

**Adopted:** 1925
**Ratio:** 3:5
**Capital:** Salem
**What it means:** The date commemorates Oregon's admission into the Union. Elements from the state seal are used. The reverse side depicts the beaver in golden yellow.

## Pennsylvania

**Adopted:** 1907
**Ratio:** 2:3
**Capital:** Harrisburg
**What it means:** The coat of arms (from 1777) features the official seal of the William Penn family, the founders of Pennsylvania.

## Rhode Island

**Adopted:** 1897
**Ratio:** 1:1
**Capital:** Providence
**What it means:** The centred anchor (symbolic of hope) has been the emblem of Rhode Island for centuries.

## South Carolina

**Adopted:** 1861
**Ratio:** 2:3
**Capital:** Columbia
**What it means:** The palmetto is the state's official tree.

## South Dakota

**Adopted:** 1963
**Ratio:** 3:5
**Capital:** Pierre
**What it means:** The state seal is depicted with the sun's rays around it. Among the elements featured in the seal are a farmer on his field, cattle, crops, a furnace and a steamship.

## Tennessee

**Adopted:** 1905
**Ratio:** 3:5
**Capital:** Nashville
**What it means:** The design and colours are based on both the Confederate battle flag and the U.S. flag.

## Texas

**Adopted:** 1839
**Ratio:** 2:3
**Capital:** Austin
**What it means:** The colours and the stripes are taken from the U.S. flag – blue for loyalty, white for strength, and red for bravery

## Utah

**Adopted:** 1913
**Ratio:** 2:3
**Capital:** Salt Lake City
**What it means:** 1847 was the year when the first Mormon settlers came to Salt Lake City. 1896 marked Utah's joining the Union as the 45th state. The beehive is symbolic of industry. Sego lilies, the state flower, stand for peace.

## Vermont

**Adopted:** 1923
**Ratio:** 3:5
**Capital:** Montpelier
**What it means:** The coat of arms pictures the Green Mountains in the background, with a large pine tree, a cow and sheaves of wheat in the foreground. A stag's head is at the crest.

## Virginia

**Adopted:** 1861
**Ratio:** 7:11
**Capital:** Richmond
**What it means:** The state seal features a woman dressed as an ancient warrior, wearing a helmet and holding a spear and sword. She is standing over the figure of a tyrant lying on the ground. The Latin motto reads: "Thus always to tyrants."

## Washington

**Adopted:** 1923
**Ratio:** 2:3
**Capital:** Olympia
**What it means:** The state seal bears the name of the state, the date of admission into the Union, and a bust of George Washington, the first president of the U.S.A.

## West Virginia

**Adopted:** 1929
**Ratio:** 10:19
**Capital:** Charleston
**What it means:** The seal has a farmer and a mountaineer standing on either side of a rock with the date when West Virginia was admitted into the Union.

## Wisconsin

**Adopted:** 1913
**Ratio:** 2:3
**Capital:** Madison
**What it means:** The date recalls the attainment of statehood. The U.S. motto "One out of many" and the national shield are inscribed at the centre.

## Wyoming

**Adopted:** 1917
**Ratio:** 2:3
**Capital:** Cheyenne
**What it means:** The white bison carries the 1893 state seal. The seal depicts a rancher and a miner. The woman represents equal rights.

## District of Colombia

**Adopted:** 1938
**Ratio:** 10:19
**Capital:** Washington D.C.
**What it means:** The design was based on the shield from the coat of arms used by the Washington family.

# CANADA

T he northernmost country in North America, Canada also makes up nearly two-fifths of the continent. The country occupies an area of 9,984,670 square kilometres (3,855,103 square miles).

1 Yukon Territory
2 British Columbia
3 Northwest Territories
4 Alberta
5 Saskatchewan
6 Nunavut
7 Manitoba
8 Ontario
9 Quebec
10 Newfoundland and Labrador
11 Prince Edward Island
12 New Brunswick
13 Nova Scotia

## Alberta

**Adopted:** 1968
**Ratio:** 1:2
**Capital:** Edmonton
**What it means:** The St George Cross recalls the region's English settlement.

## British Columbia

**Adopted:** 1960
**Ratio:** 3:5
**Capital:** Victoria
**What it means:** Features an extended Union Jack in the upper half, with a golden crown at the centre.

## Northwest Territories

**Adopted:** 1969
**Ratio:** 1:2
**Capital:** Yellowknife
**What it means:** Blue is symbolic of the skies and waters in the territory, and white of the ice and snow.

## Prince Edward Island

**Adopted:** 1964
**Ratio:** 2:3
**Capital:** Charlottetown
**What it means:** Based on a banner featuring the 1905 coat of arms.

## Manitoba

**Adopted:** 1966
**Ratio:** 1:2
**Capital:** Winnipeg
**What it means:** The coat of arms bears a bison (a source of food and clothing) and the Cross of St George.

## Nova Scotia

**Adopted:** 1929
**Ratio:** 3:4
**Capital:** Halifax
**What it means:** Based on the royal arms of Scotland and the Scottish St Andrew Cross (with the colours reversed).

## Quebec

**Adopted:** 1948
**Ratio:** 2:3
**Capital:** Québec City
**What it means:** Each of the quarters bear a fleur-de-lys (flowers), which has historic associations with France.

## New Brunswick

**Adopted:** 1965
**Ratio:** 5:8
**Capital:** Fredericton
**What it means:** The golden lion in the upper red stripe is believed to recall the region's ties with England.

## Nunavut

**Adopted:** 1999
**Ratio:** 9:16
**Capital:** Iqaluit
**What it means:** The traditional *inuksuk* at the centre represents stone markers that guide people on land.

## Saskatchewan

**Adopted:** 1962
**Ratio:** 1:2
**Capital:** Regina
**What it means:** The prairie lily is the official floral emblem of the province.

## Newfoundland and Labrador

**Adopted:** 1980
**Ratio:** 1:2
**Capital:** Saint John's
**What it means:** The two red-outlined triangles represent the mainland and the islands.

## Ontario

**Adopted:** 1965
**Ratio:** 1:2
**Capital:** Toronto
**What it means:** This was the first flag in Canada to feature the maple leaf.

## Yukon Territory

**Adopted:** 1967
**Ratio:** 1:2
**Capital:** Whitehorse
**What it means:** At the centre are the coat of arms and the territory's floral emblem.

# UNITED KINGDOM

Great Britain – comprising England, Wales and Scotland – and Northern Island are together called the United Kingdom. It is an island country located off the northwestern coast of the European mainland. With the exception of the land border with the Republic of Ireland, the United Kingdom is surrounded by sea – the North Sea, the English Channel, the Celtic Sea, the Irish Sea and the Atlantic Ocean.

### Alderney

**Adopted:** 1906
**Ratio:** 3:5
**Capital:** St Anne
**What it means:** Features the Cross of St George and the coat of arms.

### England

**Adopted:** 1277
**Ratio:** 3:5
**Capital:** London
**What it means:** The Cross of St George is featured against a white field.

### Guernsey

**Adopted:** 1962
**Ratio:** 2:3
**Capital:** St Peter Port
**What it means:** The gold cross sets it apart from the flag of England.

### Isle of Man

**Adopted in:** 1971
**Ratio:** 1:2
**Capital:** Douglas
**What it means:** Features the symbol of *triskelion*, which is believed to be based on an ancient Sun symbol.

### Jersey

**Adopted:** 1981
**Ratio:** 3:5
**Capital:** St Helier
**What it means:** The coat of arms and crown is featured at the top.

### Northern Ireland

**Adopted:** 1953
**Ratio:** 1:2
**Capital:** Belfast
**What it means:** This flag ceased to be official in 1973. The Union Jack is currently used as the official flag.

### Sark

**Adopted:** 1938
**Ratio:** 3:5
**Capital:** L'Ecluse
**What it means:** Incorporates the Cross of St George. The red canton features two yellow lions.

### Scotland

**Adopted:** 1512
**Ratio:** 3:5
**Capital:** Edinburgh
**What it means:** The Cross of St Andrew is in honour of the patron saint of Scotland.

### Wales

**Adopted:** 1959
**Ratio:** 3:5
**Capital:** Cardiff
**What it means:** The Red Dragon has long been an emblem for the Welsh people.

# INTERNATIONAL
# FLAGS

### Arab League

Features the emblem of the league, which currently comprises 22 Arab states.

### ASEAN

The flag of the Association of Southeast Asian Nations represents the main colours of the flags of the 10 member nations.

### CARICOM

The yellow circle in the centre of the flag represents the sun, bearing the logo of the Caribbean Community and Common Market, founded in 1973.

### CIS

The Commonwealth of Independent States is a confederation of 12 countries belonging to the former Soviet Union.

### Commonwealth

The logo of the Commonwealth of Nations features the letter C about a representation of the globe.

### European Union

The 12 gold stars symbolise the union of the peoples of European countries.

### NATO

The North Atlantic Treaty Organization is an international defence alliance, meant chiefly for countries in Europe and North America.

### OAS

The Organization of American States is an association of nearly all the independent countries in North America, Central America and South America

### OAU (African Union)

The coat of arms is featured in the centre.

### OIC

The flag of the Organization of the Islamic Conference features pan-Arab colours and the inscription 'Allahu Akbar', meaning 'God is great.'

### Olympic Movement

The five interlocked rings were incorporated to represent the 'five parts of the world' in which the games were pursued actively.

### OPEC

The Organization of Petroleum Exporting Countries was set up to coordinate petroleum-related policies of oil-producing nations.

### Pacific Community

The stars stand for the member countries.

### Red Cross

The International Movement of the Red Cross and Red Crescent is a humanitarian agency. Its flag features the well known symbols of mercy and complete neutrality.

### United Nations

The flag depicts a map of the Earth flanked by two olive branches – an apt logo for a peacekeeping organisation.

# SIGNAL
# FLAGS

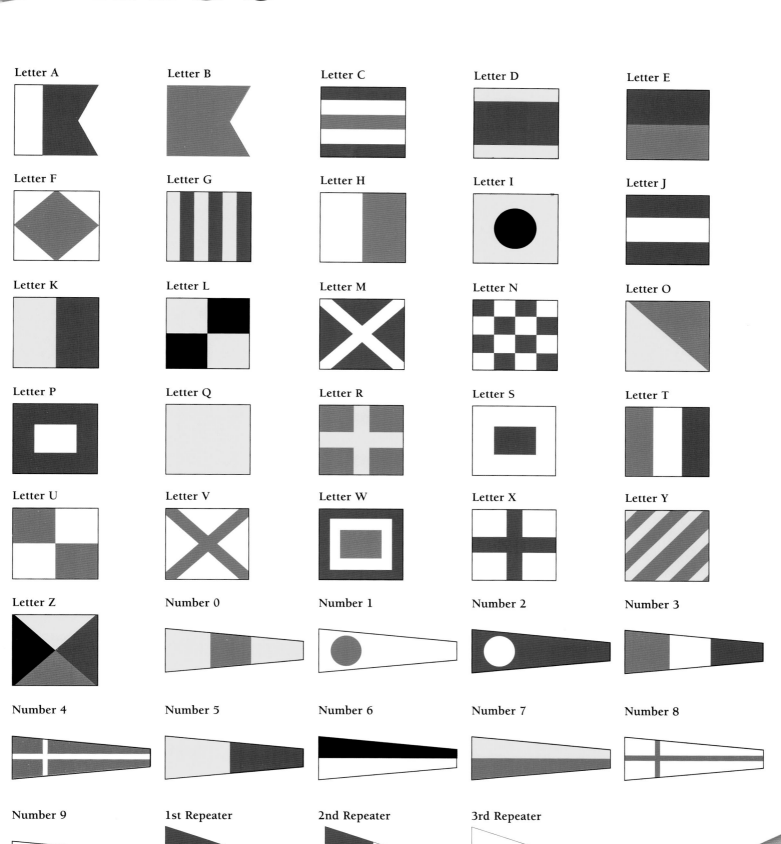

Letter A

Letter B

Letter C

Letter D

Letter E

Letter F

Letter G

Letter H

Letter I

Letter J

Letter K

Letter L

Letter M

Letter N

Letter O

Letter P

Letter Q

Letter R

Letter S

Letter T

Letter U

Letter V

Letter W

Letter X

Letter Y

Letter Z

Number 0

Number 1

Number 2

Number 3

Number 4

Number 5

Number 6

Number 7

Number 8

Number 9

1st Repeater

2nd Repeater

3rd Repeater

# SECTION

# TYPES OF FLAGS

Match the given type of flags on this page with the specific flags on the opposite page. Find out which shapes and designs are more commonly used!

**1. BORDER**

**2. BICOLOUR**

**3. SALTIRE**

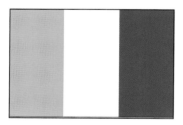

**4. TRICOLOUR**

**5. COUPED CROSS**

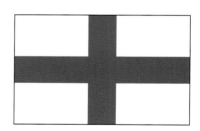

**6. CROSS**

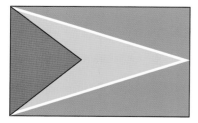

**7. FIMBRIATION**

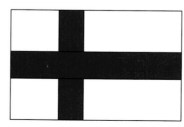

**8. SCANDINAVIAN CROSS**

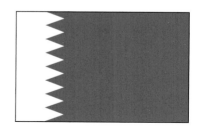

**9. SERRATION**

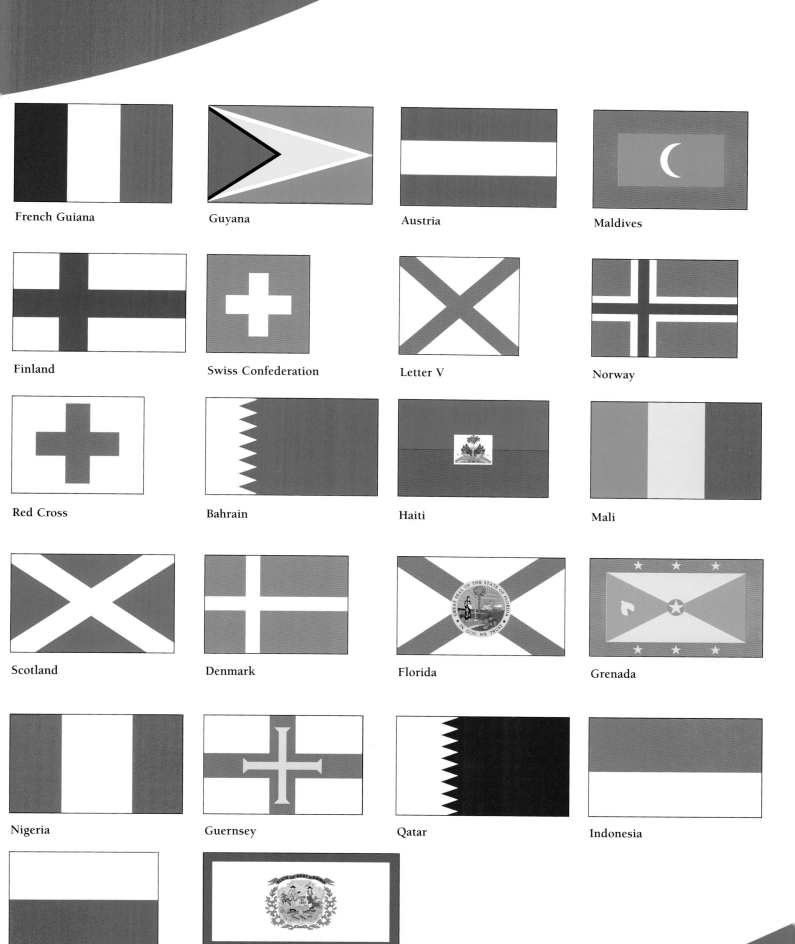

French Guiana

Guyana

Austria

Maldives

Finland

Swiss Confederation

Letter V

Norway

Red Cross

Bahrain

Haiti

Mali

Scotland

Denmark

Florida

Grenada

Nigeria

Guernsey

Qatar

Indonesia

Poland

West Virginia

# INDEX

ARCTIC OCEAN

GREENLAND
(DENMARK)

ALASKA
(USA)

ICELAND        Faero Islands
(DENMARK)

CANADA

IRELAND    UNITED
KINGDOM

FRA

UNITED STATES OF AMERICA

ATLANTIC OCEAN

Azores
(PORTUGAL)

PORTUGAL    SPAIN

PACIFIC OCEAN

Madeira
(PORTUGAL)

Gibraltar
(UK)

MOROCCO

TROPIC OF CANCER

Canary
Islands
(SPAIN)

WESTERN
SAHARA

ALGE

Hawaiian
Islands (USA)

MEXICO

BAHAMAS

CUBA
JAMAICA
BELIZE
HAITI
GUATEMALA    HONDURAS
EL SALVADOR    NICARAGUA
Ile Clipperton
(FRANCE)

DOMINICAN
REPUBLIC
13    1
CARIBBEAN
SEA
11  12

Cape
Verde

MAURITANIA

MAL

2
3
4
5
6   8
9  7
10

SENEGAL
GAMBIA
GUINEA-BISSAU    GUINEA

SIERRA LEONE
LIBERIA

BURKINA
FASO

IVORY
COAST

GHANA

COSTA
RICA
PANAMA

VENEZUELA

GUYANA

SURINAM

FRENCH GUIANA

Coco Island
(COSTA RICA)

COLOMBIA

EQUATOR                                                                    EQUATOR

ECUADOR

Marquesas Islands
(FR POLY)

Galapagos
Islands
(ECUADOR)

PERU

BRAZIL

Tuamotu
Islands
(FR POLY)

FRENCH
POLYNESIA

BOLIVIA

Pitcairn (UK)

Isla San
Ambrosio
(CHILE)

PARAGUAY

TROPIC OF CAPRICORN

Easter Island
(CHILE)

CHILE

Archipelago
Juan Fernandez
(CHILE)

URUGUAY

ARGENTINA

Falkland
Islands
(UK)

South Georgia (UK)

ANTARCTIC CIRCLE